Changing the
Way We Prepare
Educational Leaders

Changing the Way We Prepare Educational Leaders

The Danforth Experience

Mike M. Milstein
and Associates

CORWIN PRESS, INC.
A Sage Publications Company
Newbury Park, California

For information address:

Corwin Press, Inc.
A Sage Publications Company
2455 Teller Road
Newbury Park, California 91320

SAGE Publications Ltd.
6 Bonhill Street
London EC2A 4PU
United Kingdom

SAGE Publications India Pvt. Ltd.
M-32 Market
Greater Kailash I
New Delhi 110 048 India

Printed in the United States of America

Library of Congress Cataloging-in-Publication Data

Changing the way we prepare educational leaders : the Danforth experience / by Mike M. Milstein and associates.
    p. cm.
  Includes bibliographical references and index.
  ISBN 0-8039-6077-8. — ISBN 0-8039-6078-6 (pbk.)
  1. School administrators—Training of—United States. 2. School principals—Training of—United States. 3. School management and organization—United States. 4. Educational leadership—United States. 5. Danforth Foundation (Saint Louis, Mo.) I. Milstein, Mike M.
LB1738.5.C43 1993   93-22350
371.2'011—dc20   CIP

The paper in this book meets the specifications for permanence of the American National Standards Institute and the National Association of State Textbook Administrators.

93 94 95 96 97 10 9 8 7 6 5 4 3 2 1

Corwin Press Production Editor: Tara S. Mead

Contents

Preface

This book is intended to be of help to those who are trying to change educational-administration preparation programs in ways that make them more relevant to the roles these leaders play. Even a casual observer of the reform scene over the past decade must realize that the demand for change and improvement in the education of coming generations represents a significant and unprecedented challenge to our educational system. These challenges call for strong and creative leadership. This, in turn, calls for a reconceptualization of how educational leaders are prepared.

In support of this important objective, the book summarizes the learnings gained since 1987 by universities that have joined the Danforth Foundation in its efforts to stimulate new approaches to the training of educational leaders. These learnings must be shared because we are at a turning point in the preparation of educational administrators. In fact, we are at the front end of a third wave in the way we think about and go about the business of preparing leaders for our schools. During the first wave, which dominated the first half of the 20th century, retired school administrators constituted the faculty of universities that had preparation programs. Their concept of training was, in large part, to share their views of the profession by

exploring events and situations that they encountered as administrators (National Society for the Study of Education, 1964).

The second wave, which began in the 1950s, is presently encoun-
tering severe criticism. It was an effort to improve training by filling
faculty ranks of preparation programs with behavioral-science
trained individuals, many of whom had little or no experience as
school administrators. The idea was that these faculty members
would use their disciplinary knowledge to do research, create a
"science" of educational administration, and share this knowledge
and insights with their students. The idea was that program graduates
would then have a thorough grounding in theory that could be
applied to administrative situations.

The reality is that the pendulum shifted so far from retired
practitioners with little, if any, conceptual basis in training novices, to
faculty members who espoused theory but typically gave little emphasis to helping potential leaders learn their craft by providing
opportunities for carefully supervised and practical clinical experiences. As a result, as Murphy and Hallinger (1987) note,

> Practitioners have become disillusioned by the failure of
> university programs to ground training procedures in the
> realities of the workplace and by their reluctance to treat
> content viewed as useful by administrators. This disenchant-
> ment, in turn, is partially fueling the demand for changes in
> methods of training school administrators. (p. 252)

Supporting this conclusion, a survey of preparation program
graduates by Heller, Conway, and Jacobson (1988) found that 51% of
1,123 respondents rated their graduate training in educational administration as only fair or poor. Forty-six percent thought that their
preparation programs were not rigorous enough for the realities of
the positions for which they were training. Most devastating, when
asked what the most significant element in their preparation was,
only 10% identified their graduate program, as opposed to more than
60% who identified on-the-job training.

The growing criticisms about shortcomings in the preparation of
administrators culminated in a major review of the situation by the

University Council for Educational Administration (UCEA), an organization that is composed of more than 50 leading university-based preparation programs. The report that emanated from this review, *Leaders for America's Schools* (UCEA, 1987), provided a much-needed impetus for the third wave. The report concluded that preparation programs were in need of major changes. The report suggested that programs should seek to meet criteria such as the following:

- Define effective educational leadership
- Recruit high-quality candidates who have the potential to become future leaders
- Develop collaborative relationships with school-district leaders
- Encourage ethnic minorities and women to enter the field
- Promote continuing professional development for practicing administrators
- Redesign preparation programs so that they are sequential, updated in content, and include meaningful clinical experiences

In short, by the second half of the 1980s, there was a growing consensus that preparation programs needed to be reconceptualized if they were to be relevant to the job demands of educational leaders.

At the height of the discussion, the Danforth Foundation decided to apply its resources to challenge universities to change the way they prepare educational leaders in ways that are more responsive to school districts' leadership needs. This decision led to the Danforth Programs for the Preparation of School Principals (DPPSP), which began with four universities in 1987 and was expanded to include 22 universities by 1992.

It is important to summarize what has been learned as a result of these experimental program efforts, because the efforts have implications for the approximately 500 higher-education institutions that prepare educational administrators, many of which are struggling to increase the relevance of their preparation programs. To establish outcomes of these efforts, the foundation initiated two studies. The first study consisted of a survey to gather basic information about the program efforts at all of the participating universities. The results of this study, which was conducted between 1990 and 1991, have been disseminated to unit heads of preparation programs throughout the country.

The second study consists of case analyses of five preparation programs that are part of the Danforth effort. Initially, all participating programs were divided into three regions of the country. Each was visited for a day or two by a regional coordinator—Bruce Barnett of Northern Colorado University in the west, Donn Gresso of East Tennessee University in the south, and David Parks of Virginia Tech in the east—to get a sense of the situation at each institution. Subsequently, the three regional coordinators met with Peter Wilson, who is responsible for the foundation's DPPSP, and Mike Milstein of the University of New Mexico, who later conducted the case studies, to agree on the five programs to include in the study. Selection criteria comprised (a) significant progress toward the development of an effective field-based program; (b) inclusion of both newer (2 years) and older (4 or 5 years) programs; (c) representation of institutions from different parts of the country; and (d) involvement by both rural and urban universities.

Results of the initial site visits were shared and measured against the agreed-upon criteria. As a result, the following five universities were selected as case-study settings:

> *The University of Alabama*—A member of the first cycle of Danforth-funded institutions, Alabama is the longest continuing program in the case-study group. It serves a statewide constituency that includes both rural and urban school districts. The faculty decided to experiment with an alternative program design because it believed that national and state pressures for reform called for a different approach to leadership training.
>
> *Central Florida University*—A member of the fifth cycle of Danforth-funded institutions, Central Florida has had continuing turnover of its program leadership and is still experimenting with and modifying its new program design. The university serves the metropolitan Orlando, Florida, area. With this turnover, there was little ownership of or commitment to the status quo offerings that preceded the

new program approach, so advocates of change found little resistance to their proposals.

The University of Connecticut—A member of the fourth cycle of participating institutions, the program serves the school districts in the Hartford metropolitan area. Many difficulties were initially encountered by the would-be program-change agents. After an initial false start, the program was reconceptualized, and it is now in high demand.

California State University at Fresno—A member of the fifth Danforth programs cycle, the university serves Fresno and the rural agricultural communities of California's Central Valley. The arrival of a faculty member who had previously participated in the design of a Danforth-sponsored program at another institution provided the impetus for program reform at Fresno. The program has progressed so rapidly that it is already completing its third cohort.

The University of Washington—A member of the second cycle of Danforth-related programs, the university initially offered the new program to school districts from the metropolitan Seattle area, but it has since expanded its intake to include rural districts in Washington State. The university won a prestigious national award for its status quo program the very same year that it chose to review and change its approach to leadership training in education.

After agreeing to participate in the study, each institution provided the case writer with documents to give him an initial understanding of the program. These included such documents as planning and program designs, brochures, student demographic statistics, program evaluation summaries, and papers prepared for presentation or publication.

Each preparation program was visited for approximately 1 week, some time between February and June of 1992. During the visit, interviews were held with program coordinators, faculty members, university administrators, a sample of students and program alumni, site supervisors, and school-district leaders. Visits were made to academic class sessions and reflective seminars, as well as to interns' field sites. Other events were observed as possible (e.g., an orientation session for new students at Alabama, a planning meeting between the coordinator and a key superintendent at Fresno, and a dinner honoring site supervisors at Washington). Results of the visits were drafted and shared with program coordinators and other faculty members, to be certain that facts were recorded accurately. Later drafts were reviewed by the foundation's regional coordinators and by Peter Wilson, as a second check on accuracy and completeness.

Organization of the Book

The book is divided into nine chapters. The first chapter, by Donn Gresso, who was the initial DPPSP director, describes the thinking behind the foundation's efforts and the process that was devised to create and maintain foundation/university partnerships. Chapter 2, by Paula Cordeiro, Jo Ann Krueger, David Parks, Nan Restine, and Peter Wilson, presents a summary of the survey of all Danforth-related preparation programs. Chapters 3 through 8, by Mike Milstein, include the results of the five case studies and a synthesis of what was learned overall. Finally, Chapter 9, by Peter Wilson, explores the ramifications of what has been learned and points toward future issues and directions for educational leadership of this nation's schools and colleges of education.

The book is the culmination of a project that has required the involvement and assistance of many individuals. Among these are some whose insights and efforts should be particularly recognized. Peter Wilson persuaded the Danforth Foundation to support the effort. Bruce Barnett, Donn Gresso, and David Parks made preliminary site visits, played key roles in identifying the case-study settings, and provided, along with Peter Wilson, valuable feedback on drafts of the cases. The program coordinators and unit heads at each university contributed freely of their time and knowledge. These coordinators and unit heads include Maria Shelton and Jerry Herman at Alabama, Marie Hill and Bill Bozeman at Central Florida, Paula Cordeiro and Mark Shibles at Connecticut, Don Coleman (who is both coordinator and unit head) at Fresno, and Kathy Mueller and Ken Sirotnik at Washington. Melissa Sanchez edited the final manuscript.

If errors remain, they exist despite the good efforts of these people and are the sole responsibility of the authors.

MIKE M. MILSTEIN
Albuquerque, New Mexico

References

Heller, R., Conway, J., & Jacobson, S. (1988, September). Executive educator survey. *The Executive Educator*, pp. 18-22.

Murphy, J., & Hallinger, P. (1987). *Approaches to administrative training in education.* Albany: State University of New York Press.

National Society for the Study of Education. (1964). *Behavioral science and educational administration.* Chicago: University of Chicago Press.

University Council for Educational Administration. (1987). *Leaders for America's schools: The report of the National Commission on Excellence in Educational Administration.* Tempe, AZ: Author.

About the Authors

Paula A. Cordeiro is Assistant Professor of Educational Administration at the University of Connecticut. Since receiving her degree in 1990 from the University of Houston, her research has focused on preparation of principals and on school administration in culturally diverse settings. A former English-as-a-second-language (ESL) teacher and principal in American/International Schools in Venezuela and Spain, she now facilitates the University of Connecticut's principal-preparation program and teaches graduate courses in supervision and administration.

Donn W. Gresso is Associate Professor of Educational Leadership and Policy Analysis at East Tennessee State University. With varied experiences in the public schools as teacher and administrator, followed by philanthropic work as Vice President of the Danforth Foundation, he has placed emphasis on the study of human personal and professional development. At present, his writing is focused on improving the quality of instruction and experiences presented by university professors and adjunct partners for aspiring school leaders.

Jo Ann Krueger directs the internship programs in educational administration at the University of New Mexico, where she also teaches courses in school law and problem solving in educational organizations. After receiving her Ph.D. in educational administration in 1975, she entered the practitioner ranks of school administrators. While serving as high school principal, her school was recognized for its excellence and effectiveness by the U.S. Department of Education. During her school principalship, she was named "Secondary Principal of the Year" in New Mexico by the state's Association of Secondary School Principals and the New Mexico School Administrators Association and nationally by the National Association of Secondary School Principals. She joined the faculty of educational administration at the University of New Mexico in 1989. She is the deputy director of the North Central Association for New Mexico. Her research interests include mentoring, field supervision, leadership, and adult learning. She serves as the editor of *Connections*, the national newsletter for the Danforth Principals Preparation Network.

Mike M. Milstein, Professor of Educational Administration at the University of New Mexico, played a key role in the development of that program's innovative approaches to administrative internships. Prior to this position, he was a professor of educational administration at SUNY/Buffalo. His teaching, research, and writing interests are in the area of organization development. Most recently, he has focused his research on (a) school restructuring and (b) manifestations and costs of educator plateauing and ways in which individuals and organizations can respond to it more effectively.

David Parks is Associate Professor of Education at Virginia Polytechnic Institute and State University, where he serves as a cofacilitator of the Danforth-supported principals' preparation program. Since completing the doctorate at Syracuse University, he has maintained a teaching interest in administrative theory and close connections with practitioners through the development of personnel evaluation systems and field-based preparation programs. His recent writings and presentations have focused on personnel evaluation, morale, leadership, and principal preparation. Forthcoming through the National Policy Board for Educational Administration is *Defining the Cultural* *and Philosophical Values Performance Domain (for Educational Leaders),* which he prepared with Jim Garrison of Virginia Tech and Mary Jane Connelly of the University of Tennessee.

Nan Restine is Assistant Professor of Educational Administration and Higher Education at Oklahoma State University. Since receiving her Ph.D. in 1990 from the University of New Mexico, her focus of interest and inquiry has been in the areas of professional preparation of educational administrators, adult development, internships, and experiential learning. She is the coauthor of *Internship Programs in Educational Administration: A Guide to Preparing Educational Leaders* (1991) with Mike Milstein and Bettye Bobroff. She is currently conducting a study of the relationships of informal systems and mentoring processes in organizations.

Peter T. Wilson is Program Director at the Danforth Foundation in St. Louis. He has primary responsibility for the foundation's activity in the area of school leadership. His major interests are in developing inclusive, democratic, learner-centered schools, based on constructivist principles. He is interested in the development of moral leadership, teacher empowerment, and the collaboration of school, community, and university. Before coming to the foundation 3 years ago, he spent 17 years in the principalship. He taught elementary school in New York City and with Peace Corps Thailand. Wilson did his doctoral work at the University of Massachusetts, Amherst.

Genesis of the Danforth Preparation Program for School Principals

Donn W. Gresso

The Danforth Foundation of St. Louis, Missouri, has a long history of influencing education and educators at the precollegiate and collegiate ranks. These influences have occurred through grant awards, seminars, forums, foundation programs in partnership with school districts, state departments, colleges, and universities. Indirectly, the foundation's influence has been realized through a supporting role with other foundations, professional organizations, and independent agencies friendly toward educational advancement.

In the spring of 1985, the leadership of the foundation directed its staff to initiate planning activities, which would eventually influence the leadership of precollegiate schooling. A review of the literature at this time (1985) was not without ideas regarding what others were saying was wrong with public education in America. However, little was being written to this point about the leadership of schools. Seldom were the titles of "superintendent" and "principal" used in reform recommendations. One of the vice presidents of the foundation was very sensitive about the lack of recognition in the reform literature for the role principals play in school leadership. As the foundation staff continued to analyze reform reports, it became more obvious that change would occur if legislation, external involvement through partnerships, and teacher preparation were improved. Leadership in the change process at the district and school, however, appeared to be forgotten. It was at this point, in late 1985 and early 1986, that formal discussions and proposal writing were initiated by staff members of the foundation. The purposes of these activities were to emphasize the need for leadership in reform, and to provide school leaders able to do the job.

A Two-Pronged Plan

The foundation staff believed that the consensus and recommendations of recent reform reports were of such significant consequence that a major overhaul was about to begin in education. Therefore, the expenditure of foundation funds to remediate conditions already existent was not the best method for long-term influence. Why not initiate the reform of principal-preparation programs by seeking candidates from among highly effective classroom teachers, especially females and minorities? From the beginning, it was clear that the major players in the preparation of a new type of principal were concerned, but it appeared that no one group of stake-holders was willing to move off center on the issue of principal preparation.

Nonetheless, the foundation staff did find enough support close to St. Louis to remain enthusiastic and optimistic about making a positive contribution. Personnel in some districts geographically near the foundation expressed concern about the lack of relevancy in the way teachers were being prepared to assume positions of leadership in the school. They also believed that there was a lack of interest on the part of the faculty at the university with regard to the operational skills new principals brought to the job. A third concern was that local school district personnel wanted to share responsibility for the developmental experiences such as guided field experience, seminars, and adjunct faculty sharing field-tested techniques in school administration. Similar conversations were held with university representatives in other parts of Missouri and Illinois about their perceptions of what attributes a new principal should bring to the job in the coming decade. However, responses from university personnel were often clouded and obscured with concerns such as lack of support by the university administration, the plate is full, we cannot do any more, and we have tried cooperation with local school districts in the past, and it did not work.

Staff of the foundation tested the concerns expressed by local personnel of school districts and university faculty in the larger national network, where Danforth Foundation personnel have a long history of involvement. The responses from personnel of school districts and educational administration departments were very similar across the country with regard to the problems of getting the other parties involved in a new principal preparation program. The need to do something different than what was currently being done in the preparation of school principals was, however, an agreed-upon need.

Gene Schwilck, president of the Danforth Foundation, was an excellent resource for his staff. He was able to relate historically the efforts of the Kellogg and Ford foundations influence on school leadership-development programs. The president also described the efforts of faculty members at Butler University to pioneer field experiences through a planned internship, and foundation staff members followed up in investigating these experiences. The results proved to be very positive. After several months of data were completed, the staff of the foundation began planning strategies for the new foundation program to address principal leadership for the nation's schools.

One new program, headed by Bruce Anderson of the foundation, was to identify 15 to 20 universities that would submit proposals for the development of new preparation programs. The focus of these new programs would be on the university faculty of each educational administration department affirming the department's mission, philosophy, curriculum, and delivery. The affirmation, however, was to be influenced by an outside facilitator from another university. Funds would be provided by the foundation for travel and resource consultants to address possible implementation strategies that faculty members had identified. What proved to be a powerful influence was the cooperative sharing that occurred among universities selected for foundation funding. This program was fully focused on professors making plans for educating the new breed of principal and school administrator.

The second new program of the foundation, the Danforth Programs for the Preparation of School Principals (DPPSP), included administrator skill development and components designed to bring about a working relationship among university departments of educational administration, local school districts, and the foundation. Each was to contribute to the preparation of school principals. The university role and responsibility, in addition to offering experiences leading to certification and licensing, was to facilitate a leadership role that would bring personnel of the state department, school districts, community, and foundation together for purposes of identifying candidates for the principalship, as well as recruitment, training, and placement of successful graduates. School districts, as suppliers and consumers, were to have a more involved role in the preparation of school principals.

Both vice presidents hoped that learning experiences from each program would allow them to make modifications in order to dovetail the two programs into one foundation-sponsored program after a 5-year period. The staff believed that a 5-year period was appropriate for the two new programs to identify, recruit, inform, and support the implementation. This period of time also coincided with planned changes in leadership at the foundation, due to projected retirement and job changes. This would allow a good time to pass before pausing and reflecting on what progress had been made in 5 years. The staff decided that this would be an appropriate time to decide whether the planned impact on school administration warranted further funding.

As a program of the foundation, DPPSP did not have to justify funding on an annual basis to the foundation Trustees. However, during the 5-year implementation at 22 university sites, it was necessary for the staff to request increases in the overall program budget three times. The increases were due primarily to two events—escalated fuel prices in the late 1980s, which increased airfares, and unexpected inflationary increases, which had a drastic effect on hotel rates, meals, and materials.

During the 5 years of implementation, quantitative evaluation was not conducted. The foundation's position was that institutions best equipped for evaluation should provide research as a contribution to the partnership and thus allow limited foundation funds to be directed toward other program needs. However, even though the first universities to implement the program were research institutions whose personnel had the capability and a long history of research, they turned out to be unwilling to research their own implementation.

Qualitative assessment of an informal nature by foundation staff was the most that was expected for annual review. Reports to the Trustees each May and November were limited to expenditure reports, number of institutions implementing the program, and feedback by staff on "how things seemed to be going." Anderson commissioned the facilitators of the "Professor Program" to provide a narrative report of progress. The idea and follow-through for evaluating what had taken place in the DPPSP during the 5½ years of implementation came from university representatives in Cycle IV, who report the results of a survey of participating universities in Chapter 2, and the foundation's commissioning of the five case studies, which are also included in this book.

In summary, the Danforth Foundation created two programs. One approach was to focus on the professors who compose the educational administration departments. The other approach, explained in more detail in this chapter, was and is to learn about improving administration preparation when different agencies with vested interests work together to prepare teachers for entry into the school as principals.

Concerns That Influenced
Program Components

Following the Danforth Foundation Trustees' acceptance of a new program concept and support funding of $150,000 per year, the staff of the foundation began preparing a prospectus to circulate to institutions of higher education with departments of educational administration. This prospectus was entitled, "The Danforth Foundation Program for the Preparation of School Principals (DPPSP)." It was conceived with the following concerns clearly in mind about what was not happening in principal preparation programs:

1. There was a lack of communication and collaboration between the universities that were preparing principals for the

consumer school districts and the needs of the schools where they would be employed.

2. There was a need to recruit high-quality candidates rather than taking those who had been self-selected.

3. There was an undersupply of ethnic minorities and female candidates for the principalship.

4. Newly licensed principals had no or minimal field experience as principals prior to employment.

5. Pedagogy in the university classroom needed greater variation in approaches in order to respond to adult learning needs.

6. University departments of educational administration needed to enlarge the number of people involved in preparation programs by reaching outside to other schools in the university and to school-district personnel.

7. A curriculum audit was needed in the educational administration department to determine whether the content was relevant for the newly proposed reform initiatives and for the needs of the consumer school district(s).

Identifying Universities to Participate

Collectively, the foundation staff decided to invite university personnel who had participated in past Danforth Foundation programs to participate in the new DPPSP. Using this list of university personnel and their respective departments, inquiries were made to investigate the degree of interest in this alternative principal-preparation program. The selection of program sites was delayed because of uncertainty as to whether the programs should be awarded to institutions that were already addressing concerns cited by foundation staff, or to institutions that would be starting completely new initiatives. The final decision was made to select institutions and departments of educational administration that represented both groups—departments that already had initiated responses to the call for reform and those that were preparing to respond.

The foundation staff also decided to select a cohort of three to six departments of educational administration every 18 months. Each selection for the 18-month duration was called a "cycle." Five cycles were named from 1987 to 1991. Each department was to receive an initial $5,000 from the foundation to develop a brochure announcing its affiliation with the Danforth Foundation, to invite school districts to participate, and to offset costs of informational meetings and orientations. This also gave the Danforth staff time to weigh the commitment of the newly identified departments and their cooperating school districts. Later, each institution selected received up to $40,000 in grant funds for program implementation. Priority was placed on selecting institutions with departments of educational administration that indicated a willingness to participate and fit some of the following criteria:

Deans of education new to their location and with a history for supporting school-district partnerships and/or deans with a reputation for supporting innovation;

Geographical diversity, to bring an understanding of the likenesses and differences in approaches to principal preparation;

Multiple institution implementation in the same state to determine the degree of influence they could provide on state legislation and licensing of school principals;

Geographical location of higher education institutions near community/school districts with high concentrations of ethnic-minority populations;

University departments with demographics indicating great diversity in the age of professors, varied beliefs and values about school administration, school principals, and leadership, as determined through on-site visits by a Danforth vice president;

Urban, suburban, and rural universities available for selection in the same cycle, to enrich the sharing of ideas;

Faculty of universities that had established themselves as successful in past Danforth Foundation innovations and program grants;

Institutions with a long and rich tradition of graduating school leaders who have greatly influenced public schools and institutions of higher education; and

New institutions recently established in mushrooming population centers.

Basic Program Components

The basic components of DPPSP that each of the invited university department and feeder school districts was asked to consider included assessment, candidates, curriculum, cycle, internship, mentors, and the university/school partnership and steering committee.

ASSESSMENT

Several aspects of assessment were considered in the program. Initially, program assessment was considered for the purpose of screening out candidates. As time progressed in the implementation of the program, assessment at many sites came to be used for diagnostic purposes in planning a learning program for the candidates, as well as for screening.

Politics became a factor in the screening/assessment process. Universities found themselves with political hot potatoes when a school district nominated persons viewed as its brightest and best, only to have the university say the nominees did not qualify for entry into the department's alternative program.

In each university program, initial standards for graduate school entrance had to be met if a program of study was pursued that would lead to an advanced degree. Following graduate school acceptance of nominees, departments conducted their own assessment. In some programs, this entails a formal interview by steering committee members, candidates writing a paper on a given topic, and candidates making a formal presentation on a committee-selected topic. At some institutions, the department screening process is also supplemented by a formal assessment center experience, such as the National Association of Secondary School Principal (NASSP) Assessment Center.

The bottom line to assessment, as recommended by the foundation staff, was to find the very best candidates for leadership positions in our schools and to look beyond the traditional leadership models of the past. Many of the attributes of the new leader were not yet quantifiable, and thus, traditional assessment was not appropriate.

CANDIDATES

Much emphasis was placed on enlarging the pool of ethnic minorities and females for school districts to consider for future leadership positions. To identify the very best candidates for principalship preparation requires faculty members in departments of educational administration and school district administrators to be proactive in recruitment. In the past, teachers showed up in advanced programs of study in educational administration for reasons ranging from gaining advanced standing on the salary schedule to meeting state-certification requirements for renewal certification. This is not likely to result in a group of candidates who are motivated to participate in an intensive alternative program such as DPPSP. A strategy that seemed to bring increased numbers of female and ethnic-minority candidates for screening occurred when program announcements and applications were distributed to all teachers in a school system. These same applications requested teachers to nominate other teachers in their building who they felt had leadership qualities.

CURRICULUM

Two areas of focus were presented to university facilitators for consideration. It was hoped that curriculum for the preparation of school principals would be reviewed by representatives of school districts who would be hiring the newly prepared principals. It was also hoped that department of educational administration faculty, along with the school-district representatives, would reach consensus on learning experiences that would be reflective of requirements for the job. Foundation staff members suggested that the following topics be considered by curriculum committees: ethics, interpersonal relations, planning, speaking, writing, and facilitating.

A related aspect of curriculum suggested as a core component of the DPPSP program was the pedagogy used in the delivery of content by the professors. Heavy emphasis was placed on improving teaching techniques in the university classroom. Alternative means for learning were suggested and demonstrated by consultants.

Finally, each institution was to analyze its current curriculum with the assistance of local representatives of the cooperating school district(s). A comparison was requested by the foundation, which would allow the university to contrast its curriculum with that being advocated in the literature. Following the self-study of the curriculum, department of educational administration faculty were urged to initiate a personal- and professional-growth program for improvement. Danforth staff members suggested that each department of educational administration should study and discuss current practices and procedures being used for preparing teachers to serve as principals. Based on these discussions, plans were to be written for what steps the faculty would initiate in their own professional development and the changes the department might make in the way it operated.

CYCLE

Three to six universities participated in each cycle. Cross-institutional meetings were established for a period of 18 months, to encourage the sharing of plans and results for implementation of the components of DPPSP.

INTERNSHIP

University program facilitators were asked to schedule an internship experience for each aspiring principal candidate. The ideal internship was to be of one semester's duration in a school location other than the one in which they taught. The Danforth staff suggested that interns experience administration at the elementary, middle, and high school level during the internship. The experience was seen as one that would provide for a safe environment in which to test theory and practice. Facilitators were cautioned to look for and remove interns from experiences that were in the best interests of the school, but not in the best interests of the intern.

It was suggested that the teachers' cooperating school district provide a substitute for them when they participated in the internship. This proved to be a stumbling block in some programs. During the internship, the aspiring principal was to be guided by a mentor, the site administrator, who became the second member of the team. The third member of the internship team was the university facilitator or a member of the university department of educational administration faculty. This triad was responsible for the planned program, activities, and evaluation of each intern.

MENTORS

A part of the cooperative effort with local school districts included the identification, recruitment, and training of mentors. A great deal of interest and learning took place with this component. Several of the DPPSP facilitators working with the concept of mentoring became nationally recognized for their knowledge on this topic. Mentors in the program were to be school administrators, but others such as community leaders, public service agency leaders, CEOs in business operations, and political leaders were to be recruited. Students were encouraged to work with as many mentor leaders as possible during their internship.

UNIVERSITY/SCHOOL PARTNERSHIP
AND STEERING COMMITTEE

Each university facilitator representing the DPPSP was to orient members of the university department about components of the program. The department was to establish an ongoing working relationship with school-district representatives. Representatives from the university and school district(s) were to establish a steering committee. Membership on the steering committee was to be expanded to include representatives from the state department of education, community service organizations, business and industry, and school board(s). Meetings were to be scheduled on a regular basis for the purposes of setting an implementation agenda, feedback, evaluation, and providing information to the university, school, and community audiences. It was suggested that the university facilitator of the program convene the first meeting, and in subsequent meetings, a member of the committee would serve as chair. After the first year of operation, it was suggested that graduates and mentors of the program have representation on the steering committee.

Each university, together with its school-district partners, selected components that they believed to be appropriate for their particular situation. No one component of the DPPSP was consistently selected by the steering committees. The foundation staff members, however, believed that selection of components should be the first activity in the initiation of the program.

PROGRAM FACILITATOR

After a university department reached consensus, and approval was given by the total faculty to participate in the DPPSP, a faculty member was selected to serve as a facilitator for the program. The facilitator was to be a teaching member of the faculty and a liaison between the university department and the Danforth Foundation. The facilitator was expected to attend a number of development sessions sponsored by the foundation over an 18-month period.

Reflections on the Selection of Universities to Participate in Programs for the Preparation of School Principals

The basic premises described earlier for initial selection of departments for participation in DPPSP were appropriate. A great deal of time and effort was afforded to the members of the department faculty during the foundation's recruiting period. More time than needed was spent with university administrators to gain their approval for the department to participate. In retrospect, the university administrators' primary interests were the grant and the possibility for additional funding from the foundation. More time should have been devoted to soliciting the support of school-district(s) superintendents and school-board members.

Problems that followed with the release of classroom teachers could have been reduced if a representative of the Danforth Foundation had addressed the importance of these activities to the school boards and superintendents. This job, however, was left to a university faculty member—in many cases, to the newest member of the department, and often the newest member of the community. Solid political alliances had not yet been established between universities and school districts, so they were unable to make unified requests for school-board support of the new program. Superintendents were not always able to bring the pressure necessary to expand or redirect the district budget to include paying for a substitute to replace a teacher serving an administrative internship. A common complaint from school-board members who were not fully informed about DPPSP was that they already had teachers certified to be principals who were not given financial support by the district for leave from their classroom.

The foundation staff determined that the time line established for the program was too short, and too many universities were expected to participate, given the dollars and the time available. Initially, more time was needed to build a common understanding and a baseline of information to bring about planned change. In retrospect, it might have been better if selection had included five universities every 2½ years.

Facilitator Orientation

Following the selection of universities for participation in DPPSP, each institution selected a faculty member to represent the department at the first Danforth Foundation-sponsored orientation. This selection of the facilitator proved to be one of the most important determiners of individual program success. Again, the reality of the selection process was that the newest member of the department was typically selected or directed to be facilitator of the DPPSP. In the future, departments might instead consider selecting the faculty member having the greatest rapport with local school-district personnel and the lengthiest tenure with the university.

Orientation sessions for facilitators were conducted in St. Louis in the offices of the Danforth Foundation. The travel expenses of the facilitator were assumed by the Danforth Foundation, relieving the universities of any initial costs for participation. The first session typically was 2½ days in duration. Initial activities included the sharing of information about the university represented by each facilitator. In order to develop a feeling of a cohort, rather than a cycle of isolated universities, team building became a formal part of the 18-month program. A notebook was provided for each facilitator by the Danforth Foundation. The content included an overview of the program, and time was taken to interpret the meaning and intent of the written and verbal description of the program. Another section of the notebook contained recently published material about the principalship. This was done to provide a common base of knowledge for discussions.

After the first cycle of institutions had initiated implementation of the program, sample forms, strategies, and resources were included in the orientation notebooks for Cycles II through V. The rate at which departments of educational administration implemented program components increased with the inclusion of each new cycle of universities. Extensive sharing took place across cycles at national meetings sponsored by the Danforth Foundation. Newsletters, informal networking, and presentations at regional, state, and national conventions also strengthened the cohort concept. Following the initial orientation session in St. Louis, institutions took turns serving as hosts on their campus for the institutions in their cycle. For the training sessions, the Danforth Foundation identified and paid for resource personnel (consultants), along with travel and related expenses for each facilitator.

Other Activities
Connected With the Program

Regional meetings were initiated by participating departments of educational administration, with a mix of departments from various cycles. The Danforth Foundation also sponsored two national meetings in Point Clear, Alabama, and Norman, Oklahoma, that encompassed multiple university participation.

The foundation initiated a computer network and paid for subscriptions for each university to be connected. Lack of participation, however, forced the foundation to let the subscriptions expire. Subsequently, a national newsletter was developed in cooperation with the University of Alabama. This glossy publication provided for each institution to submit news and information about people associated with their programs and events taking place at their site. This activity was eventually transferred to the National Policy Board for School Administrators. The new publication is called *Design.* In a very short period of time, articles, monographs, and books have been written about the DPPSP experience. It is my belief that more publications will follow in the years ahead.

In Closing

Foundation funds in this country are viewed by some in the general populace as societal venture capital. Without the investment made by the Danforth Foundation Trustees in a program conceptualized in 1986 and implemented in 1987, the amount of change undertaken in the way principals are prepared would not have had an impact on so many universities at one time.

The components of the DPPSP were given an unanticipated boost when the 1988 report *Leaders for America's Schools* (Griffith, Stout, & Forsyth) was released. Identified weaknesses in administrator-preparation programs that were cited in the report were already being remediated by 22 universities that participated in DPPSP.

Professors associated with the program have developed a unique network of understanding about implementing the Danforth program components. They have also identified strategies most beneficial to the development of leaders who can determine the future direction of schooling. These same professionals who have been affiliated with DPPSP have been outstanding educators in the past: They will continue to provide leadership, as they now have a new platform and enhanced legitimacy to assist their colleagues.

The lack of extrinsic rewards for professors who risked much by implementing a new approach viewed by many of the professors as an add-on to regular responsibilities should not be forgotten. Present knowledge suggests that none of the 20-plus university facilitators of the program received additional pay from their university for the time given in initiating a new way to prepare school principals. The time required usually came on top of normal expectations for teaching, research, and service to the community.

This program had no cookbook directions or numbers to follow for implementation. Foundation staff members asked many more questions of their partners at the university than they answered. It was appropriate that each of the 22 university/school-district programs was different, even though they were introduced to the same DPPSP components. Culture, interpretation, geographical location, creativity, politics, and people will always influence the type of leaders sent into the schools. It is my personal belief that the components of the DPPSP have the potential to prepare and provide for practice of the skills, knowledge, and attitudes that will enable principals to be proactive for the upcoming decade and 21st century. The Danforth Foundation's contribution to the birth of the DPPSP seems to be an effective response to the reform initiatives of the 1980s.

Reference

Griffith, D. E., Stout, R. T., & Forsyth, P. B. (Eds.). (1988). *Leaders for America's schools: The report and papers of the National Commission on Excellence in Educational Administration.* Berkeley: McCutchan.

Taking Stock

Learnings Gleaned From Universities Participating in the Danforth Program

Paula A. Cordeiro

Jo Ann Krueger

David Parks

Nan Restine

Peter T. Wilson

Since the late 1970s, researchers and writers in educational administration have discussed the discontentment of graduates of administrator preparation programs. McCarthy, Kuh, and Beckman (1979) reported that 50% of the graduate students surveyed, representing 62 institutions, felt that their program in educational administration was not relevant to problems in the real world. In a 1982 review of state-of-the-art administrator preparation programs, Pitner commented that "improvement in [administrator] training is sorely needed" (p. 52). Hoyle (1985) found that school administrators have a multitude of complaints because they find major discrepancies between what they do and the preparation they receive. In discussing the quality of programs, he concluded, "There is an opportunity to do much better" (p. 88). In addition, numerous articles and recent reports question past assumptions about and suggest guidelines for the reform of

17

educational leadership preparation (National Association of Elementary School Principals [NAESP], 1990; National Policy Board for Educational Administration [NPBEA], 1989; UCEA, 1989). Many university programs consist of a variety of courses that often have no connecting threads. In many programs, little thought is given to effective teaching, adult learning theory, linkages with school districts, field experiences that help bridge the theory-practice gap, content closely aligned with desired outcomes, or rigorous evaluation. In fact, many programs in educational administration are not programs; they are a series of discrete courses.

There have been many calls for the restructuring of administrator preparation programs (Carnegie Forum on Education and the Economy, 1986; National Commission for Excellence in Educational Administration [NCEEA], 1987; NPBEA, 1989). Each of these reports called for clinical approaches to the preparation of school administrators and meaningful collaboration between universities and local education agencies. One response to these calls was initiated by the Danforth Foundation.

In 1986, the Danforth Foundation began providing for the revitalization of principal preparation programs. The first cycle of DPPSP began with three universities. As mentioned in the preceding chapter, each year, an additional cycle with four to six universities was added. During a 5-year period, 22 universities across the nation joined forces to overcome the mediocrity that permeated preparation programs. Each university agreed to implement programs considerably different from those they were operating. Many accepted the foundation's request to include cohorts, school-district-university collaboratives, extended internships, mentor principals, and field-based delivery. In 1989, Ubben and Fowler surveyed those universities to determine strategies used in designing and implementing programs. In 1991, the present study was undertaken in an attempt to understand the impact of the Danforth-sponsored programs and to examine the differences and similarities among the 22 field-based preparation programs.

Methodology

To document the impact of Danforth-sponsored programs, the authors developed an 18-page survey requesting information from program facilitators. Data included program status, intent, content, management, pedagogy, field experiences, mentoring, students, financial arrangements, internal and external relationships, graduate outcomes, perceived program strengths and weaknesses, and other activities and issues. Data collection began in April of 1991, when the survey was mailed to all 22 Danforth program facilitators. Of the 22 universities, 21 responded. During the summer of 1991, the survey was followed up by telephone to obtain missing information or to clarify written survey responses. A second survey of three pages was initiated in July 1991. The response rate of this second survey was 86%. Data analysis began in the fall of 1991 and was completed in 1992 (Cordeiro, Krueger, Parks, Restine, & Wilson, 1992). While several articles and papers have focused on the efforts of individual Danforth-sponsored programs (Daresh & Playko, 1989; Krueger, 1991; McQuarrie, 1989; Mueller & Kendall, 1989; Papalewis, Jordan, Cuellar, Gaulden, & Smith, 1991) and others surveyed the strategies for organizing principal-preparation programs in Cycles 1 through 3 (Ubben & Fowler, 1989), the study reported here is a result of a comprehensive survey of all DPPSPs.

Findings

After 5 years of involvement, what are the results? What impact has the Danforth Foundation had on the preparation of principals at these institutions? The data describe, rather than evaluate, the state of the art in restructuring the education of school administrators through innovative programs and suggest the directions taken when resources and support from outside the universities themselves are provided. Although the findings may be limited by the study's heavy reliance on program facilitators as data sources, the findings are important even in a descriptive sense because there are few data currently available regarding alternative programs, either as single programs or across a number of university program sites.

Findings describe the restructuring efforts taking place at 22 institutions that prepare school leaders, and the findings include the status, demographics, and procedures of programs; their content; the use of cohorts; field-based experiences or internships; mentoring; collaboration with school districts; and key strengths and issues.

STATUS OF THE PROGRAMS

Data gathered from the survey (see Table 2.1) suggest that the Danforth Foundation's effort created considerable change in program delivery in preparing school principals. All but 3 of the 21 programs are currently active; 14 are fully operational, and 4 maintain portions of their earlier configurations. Of the 3 programs not operating at the time of the survey, one (University of Houston) incorporated the Danforth learnings into its ongoing program.

Information was also obtained about the existence of alternative programs for preparing principals within departments. Nineteen universities reported that another program was operating, although the status and purposes of these programs varied. Seven sites were in the process of phasing out alternative programs maintained for transitional purposes and to accommodate students previously enrolled. In three cases, alternative programs were maintained because of the more selective admissions criteria or increased financial commitment required by the innovative programs at those sites. In three additional cases, alternative programs continued because the Danforth program was considered a demonstration program and not a replacement for the existing program.

DEMOGRAPHICS AND PROCEDURES

Each program was asked to describe its demographics and structure. At the time they were surveyed, 18 programs reported having a total of 665 former or current interns, with an average across programs of 16 interns each year. Twenty-six percent were male, and 74% were female. Ethnic data indicated that 22% of the students were African-American; 8% Hispanic-American; less than 1% Native American; 2% Asian-American; and 63% European-American.

The scheduling of courses was varied and designed to meet the needs of students who continued to work while participating in the programs. The majority of programs offered courses and seminars in the late afternoon or evening. Weekend classes were reported by six sites. Seven universities reported scheduling courses in mornings or early afternoons. One site scheduled courses and seminars as all-day sessions held once a month. Except for three programs that used the

TABLE 2.1 Selected Program Data by Location

University	Year program initiated	Ave. no. students per year	Ave. hrs. interning	Alternate program in department	Collaboration with school districts	Use of cohorts
University of Alabama	1987	17	540	Y	Y	Y
Brigham Young University	1985	17	1703	Y	Y	Y
California State, Fresno	1990	18	1520	Y	Y	Y
University of Central Florida	1990	19	350	Y	Y	Y
City College of New York	1988	59	770	Y	Y	Y
University of Connecticut	1990	4	800	Y	Y	Y
East Tennessee State	1989	9	400	Y	Y	Y
Georgia State University	1987	17	120	Y	Y	Y
University of Houston	1988	12	720	Y	Y	Y
Iowa State University	1990	18	320	Y	Y	Y
University of Massachusetts	1988	17	NA	NA	Y	Y
University of New Mexico	1987	20	570	Y	Y	Y
University of Oklahoma	1988	9	720	Y	Y	Y
The Ohio State University	1987	NA	132	Y	Y	Y
Old Dominion University	1991	15	600	Y	Y	Y
San Diego State University	1989	20	432	NA	Y	Y
University of Tennessee, Knoxville	1989	5	840	Y	Y	Y
University of Virginia	1989	12	800	Y	Y	Y
Virginia Tech University	1989	17	720	Y	Y	Y
University of Washington	1988	13	480	Y	Y	Y
Western Kentucky University	1991	NA	NA	Y	Y	Y

NOTE: Y = Yes. NA = Not Available.

quarter system, the programs operated on a semester calendar. Most programs utilized a variety of locations for classes and seminars. These included university campus sites, but in a majority of cases, classes were held in schools, staff-development centers, district central offices, and other field-based locations.

A variety of degrees and levels of administrative certification were available through the programs. Master's degree programs ranged from 30 to 60 credits and took from 12 to 30 months to complete. On average, the master's level consisted of 36 credit hours, completed over an 18-month period. Education-specialist degrees ranged from 24 to 45 credits and lasted from 15 to 24 months. Doctoral programs, both Ed.D. and Ph.D., ranged from 30 to 76 credits, the difference being attributed to programs that did not offer education-specialist degrees/certificates. Survey data also indicated that 44% of the students sought the master's degree; 17% the educational specialist degree or advanced graduate certificate; 6% the Ed.D. or Ph.D.; and 25% administrative licensure or professional certification.

CONTENT OF PROGRAMS

Program facilitators were asked to rate the importance of 77 instructional topics in their programs. Instructional topics were grouped into 17 general-content areas. A consensus of 90% rated leadership as a most important content area. This is congruent with Hoyle's (1985) discussion of a study that surveyed members of the National Council of Professors of Educational Administration (NCPEA) and the UCEA regarding the most important topics they taught. Leadership skills were found to be one of three areas of highest importance, the other two being human relations and organizational development, which were also highly rated in the Danforth survey. More than half of the programs assigned "high importance" ratings to five other content areas: supervision, planning, governmental and legal issues, technology, and public relations.

Of the 77 topics, 42 were judged to be highly important by more than half of the respondents. These topics are listed in Table 2.2, together with the percentage of programs that gave them a rating of "high importance." Considering the current topics of interest in the corporate world today, it is interesting to note several items that were

TABLE 2.2 Content Topics Rated "High in Importance" by More
Than Half of the Programs, According to Percentage
of Agreement

Topic	Percentage
Oral expression	95
Human relations and interpersonal skills	95
Problem solving	95
Supervision of teachers	95
Moral and ethical dimensions of leadership	89
Leadership theory	89
Decision making	89
Curriculum development and improvement	89
Change	84
Multicultural issues; gender issues	84
Staff and human resource development	84
Teacher evaluation	84
Group dynamics	79
Conflict management	79
Organizational culture	79
Cultural and ethnic diversity of students	79
Written expression	74
Student equity issues	74
At-risk populations	74
Curriculum reform and movements	74
Motivation theory	74
Adult learning theory	74
Students' rights	74
Computer applications for administrators	74
Organizational theory	68
Theoretical foundations of educational administration	68
Federal and state governance	68
Values	68
School policy in curriculum and instruction	68
Strategic planning	68
Curriculum evaluation	63
Learning theory and human development	63
Program planning	63

(Continued)

TABLE 2.2 (Continued)

Topic	Percentage
Program evaluation	63
Teacher and administrator liability	63
Community relations	63
Coalition building and collaboration	63
Action research	63
Student guidance and development	58
Supervision of nonteaching staff	53
Legal research	53
Parent-school relations	53

rated highly: multicultural and gender issues, group dynamics, computer applications, moral and ethical dimensions of leadership, and coalition building.

Five general content areas were not rated high by respondents: business management and administration, labor management relations, politics, administration of special programs, and job skills. Within these five areas, five specific topics were a low priority for 50% or more of the programs. These topics consisted of administration of vocational programs, collective bargaining, administration of bilingual/ESL programs, teacher organizations, and statistics. The lack of priority on these five topics may be due to several factors. For example, because 61% of the programs offered either a master's or an educational-specialist degree, statistics might be seen as a low priority in programs not leading to the doctorate. In addition, some universities were located in states where collective bargaining was illegal, and teacher organizations were not major players in their educational arenas. Also, due to demographics, it is possible that the administration of bilingual/ESL and vocational programs might not be a major concern of the populations served by those universities. Finally, depending on the types of administrator certifications offered in various states, the areas of bilingual/ESL and vocational education may require specialty-area administrator certificates.

Responsiveness to Student Needs

Programs reported the use of five general strategies that promoted responsiveness to student needs. These strategies included tailoring or adjusting program content (9 programs); allowing students to evaluate or plan (5); conducting preassessments of student needs (5); providing access to staff members or advising (5); and varying the scheduling (3). The strategies recognized the need to consider the past experiences of individual students, their current situations during program participation, and the different school environments in which they will be working after graduation. Ongoing support was clearly a key component in many programs. Individual advisors assumed support roles in most programs and modeled easy accessibility to students. Student cohorts provided another type of support system. Faculty and staff were available, as needed by students, and more formal arrangements involved scheduled visits to school fieldwork sites.

Responsiveness to Emerging Issues

Given the continuous nature of change in the educational arena, programs were also asked about strategies designed to respond to emerging issues in education and society. Overall, two general strategies were articulated: (a) faculty awareness about key issues and (b) student exposure to current issues. Programs relied on faculty to research and maintain current knowledge about key issues and then to incorporate the study and discussion of these issues into courses. In addition, programs exposed students to topical issues in a variety of ways outside of the classroom.

Seminars and panels of speakers were the most frequently mentioned formats for addressing emerging or controversial topics. Monthly sessions were reserved at some sites to focus solely on current issues. One program used a steering committee to review current literature and identify emerging issues. Another site asked students to discuss new issues they felt were controversial or likely to face them as administrators. Virginia Tech and the University of Connecticut used teleconferences to discuss issues with national experts. The University of Virginia had each intern follow five at-risk students for a year, with the purpose of finding out what types of interventions took place. Overall, there were sustained efforts by programs to make curriculum content reality based, while maintaining a sound theoretical framework.

THE COHORT FORMAT

The original program objectives set by the Danforth Foundation did not specifically require that programs have a cohort format; however, there was an expectation of collaboration with school districts in the recruitment and selection of interns. An early Danforth communication asked institutions to work "with 15 to 20 able teachers who elect to prepare for school administration by this alternative program and who are endorsed by the local school officials" (Gresso, personal communication, August 13, 1988). Although this and other communications did not specify student cohorts, all participating universities adopted a cohort format for their programs. Several programs in the survey reported that the cohort arrangement was highly conducive to principal-training models. The cohort format was also mentioned by several programs as being a mechanism to ensure program integrity. These programs felt that the cohort format provided "coherence." In addition, student cohorts provided a support system and networking opportunity for participants (Restine, 1990). When asked in an open-ended question format to describe program strengths, eight programs reported the cohort format to be a major strength. One facilitator commented, "The strength of the cohort cannot be overemphasized."

FIELD-BASED EXPERIENCES OR INTERNSHIPS

Field-based experiences or internships prevail without exception across programs as a major component of preparation. Survey data indicated that the models used for implementing field experiences vary. How each program operated, its duration, and its intensity appeared to be dependent on unique characteristics of place, personnel, funding, and other aspects of programs.

Time for Interning

Survey results suggest a broad disparity among programs in the total number of hours spent interning. Time for internships ranged from 120 hours to 1703 hours. For example, Brigham Young's program offered the most clock hours in its provision of a full-time, yearlong internship funded by school districts. Fresno State offered similar expanded internships. Others, such as the University of New Mexico (UNM), provided one third of each week over a year's time for its administrative internships. Funding at UNM was based on special contractual arrangements with each cooperating school district. Still other programs used several strategies within their programs to provide half-time internships. For example, the University of Washington collaborated with school districts to arrange for lengthy internships on the basis of individual interns' circumstances and district capabilities.

The average duration of field experiences was 632 hours, the equivalent of nearly one half of a regular school year. The average falls short of the 1 year recommended by the NPBEA (1989). However, the average length of Danforth internships is twice the minimum average required by institutions within the UCEA. Paulter (1990) found that UCEA institutions required an average of 280 minimum clock hours for internships. The reported range among UCEA institutions was between 100 and 800-plus hours.

Strategies for Providing Released Time for Interning

Because most Danforth interns were also full-time educators, they could expect only peripheral administrative responsibilities unless they were systematically released from their respective responsibilities for internship experiences. Facilitators of programs agreed that time spent interning was related to the quality of administrative preparation; therefore, the programs mounted sustained efforts to achieve as much release time for interns as possible.

The success of those efforts varied along with the strategies devised. Some programs utilized more than one strategy to achieve the release of students for intern experiences. Others used different strategies at different times. Still, four major clusters were apparent in the analysis of the survey data: (a) release time funded by school districts, (b) release time funded by students, (c) release time funded by university programs, and (d) release time without funding arrangements and gained through cooperative arrangements or special student initiatives.

Nearly half (48%) of the programs provided release time through funding by local school districts that were convinced that long-term benefits may be gained by substantial investment in the preparation of future school administrators. Arrangements for district funding included, for example, interns being paid full-time and released full- or part-time for interning. Another 17% obtained release time through student funding. Arrangements for student funding included students taking part-time leave with concomant reductions in pay or students paying for substitutes through contractual arrangements with the school districts. University programs funded 3% of the strategies cited, while nearly one third (31%) involved no funding at all and depended on cooperative arrangements among school districts, universities, and students to provide release time for internships. Cooperative arrangements for release time included using student-teacher interns as substitutes, placing interns in nonclassroom positions, making up release time later, interning during summer or intersessions, and interning during nonclassroom time.

Whatever the duration of internships or strategies for gaining release time for interning, each program appeared committed to internships as a major mechanism for instruction and learning. When asked to give the rationale underlying their commitment, most program facilitators emphasized that internships provide a powerful link between theory and practice. They said, for example, that an internship or field experience:

- Provides students with as many opportunities as possible to link theory with practice (Virginia Tech)
- Helps the intern wed the knowledge base in educational administration with practice (University of New Mexico)
- Provides an opportunity to tie theory to practice (San Diego State)

- Is one of the best strategies for bridging the gap between theory and practice (Brigham Young University)

Facilitators also related that internships provide opportunities for developing important administrative skills. In the uncertain arena of administrative practice, facilitators suggest that interns begin to see relationships more clearly between the tasks at hand and skills in communication, problem solving, and conflict resolution. The University of Alabama wrote, "The internship experience permits students to implement learned skills." The University of Houston said that their internship was "designed as an integrating experience, an opportunity . . . to practice those skills and competencies learned in classroom settings and to learn certain skills best taught in a school setting." Recent research affirms the view that skill development is an important aspect of field experiences and suggests that administrative internships are an "ideal mode" for developing skills needed by school leaders (Ashe, Haubner, & Troisi, 1991).

MENTORING

Hills (1975) suggested that internships in administration should be taken far more seriously now than in the past because internships are the only contexts that influence beliefs, attitudes, and values that make the difference between moderately and outstandingly successful administrative performance. One critical condition, Hills added, was the administrator with whom the intern served and formed a close association. Nearly 2 decades later, that "close association" is called a "mentoring relationship" (Bova & Phillips, 1984; Kram, 1985) and continues to be viewed as crucial in the preparation of school principals (Barnett, 1990; Daresh, 1988).

Danforth preparation programs see the practitioners with whom interns serve, and with whom they form close associations, as significant keys to productive learning experiences for interns. When university preparation programs formed collaborative arrangements with local school districts, they joined others who recognized the importance of mentoring relationships. The partners in Danforth programs believe that if they can select a cadre of successful practitioners who willingly bond with, model for, and demonstrate to talented novices the best of administrative practice, their mutual enterprise can have a remarkable likelihood of success. Implementing the conditions is another matter. The selection, training, and evaluation of mentors remain major challenges for these programs.

Selection of Mentors

Survey data show that selection criteria and selection processes for mentors varied less among programs than did other facets of Danforth programs. Despite minor differences, the criteria for becoming a mentor included (1) success as an effective school administrator, (b) ability to share skills and knowledge with a novice, and (c) the personal and professional interest in doing so. Several programs added the stipulation that prospective mentors must attend workshops for training mentors.

Danforth programs use either of two procedures for selecting mentors: (a) joint selection by school districts and universities or (b) selection by school districts only. Nine of the responding programs select mentors jointly. For example, one program responded, "The university program staff works jointly with the school districts, usually superintendent level personnel, to ensure the best possible placement of interns with effective school leaders." Another said that the selection of mentors took place in "consultation with planning team representatives from cooperating school districts."

School districts selected mentors at eight sites. For example, the University of Houston described its process as, "The steering committee sets criteria, but school districts select mentors." The City College of New York wrote, "Mentors are chosen by the superintendents of each district, which uses its own specific criteria." California State at Fresno also indicated that mentors were "selected by districts." A small minority of programs (6%) said that mentors are selected by students themselves, together with the approval of the university program director.

Training of Mentors

Almost all of the programs (94%) featured mentor-training workshops for the practitioners who work with interns. Five programs published their own mentor handbooks or mentor-training manuals. The extent of training varied from single half-day sessions held early in the school year to eight sessions held over a year's time. Consultants and other outside agencies were occasionally used for conducting the mentor-training workshops. The following remarks were representative of various approaches to mentor training:

> The University of Alabama held "a half day session devoted to working with supervising principals at the end of the summer and prior to beginning the fall semester internship."
>
> The University of Washington provided an "orientation meeting, three sessions during the year, and four follow-up seminars for mentors on current issues."
>
> The University of Connecticut reported that it has a handbook guide for mentors and also "pays for any mentor who wants to attend the mentor training offered by the state department of education."

Some program facilitators felt that there is never enough training for mentors. The University of Houston provided a full day of training for mentors at the beginning of the program and, in retrospect, remarked, "It was not nearly enough." East Tennessee State related that they held two sessions to discuss mentoring philosophies, provided research materials, and reviewed mentoring notebooks, then supplemented the formal training events with ongoing discussions at school sites throughout the year.

Evaluation of Mentors

Given the emphasis placed on selecting and training mentors and the collective agreement among program facilitators about the importance of the mentoring relationship, the minimal effort toward evaluating mentors is surprising. Survey data show a lack of school-district involvement with either formal or informal evaluation of mentors, and only 5 of the 22 programs have formal procedures for evaluating mentors. When the evaluation of mentors takes place systematically, however, it is usually university supervisors or interns who undertake the task. "University professors evaluate mentors," answered

Iowa State University. Both Brigham Young and the University of Virginia reported that interns and supervisors from the university evaluate mentors.

For the most part, however, mentors are evaluated informally. One facilitator, for example, described the process as "very informal," while another commented, "We could be stronger in this area." These responses suggest one of two situations. Either informal processes for evaluating mentors are satisficing (i.e., satisfactorily meeting minimal criteria) as currently configured, or the evaluation of mentors is a sensitive juncture between collaborating institutions and thus remains an issue to be resolved.

COLLABORATION WITH SCHOOL DISTRICTS
AND OTHER AGENCIES

Respondents reported collaborating with teachers, principals, and a variety of central-office personnel within school districts. At the state and regional levels, collaboration occurred with state departments of education, principal associations, and regional service and assessment centers. Other agencies involved with Danforth programs included business organizations, youth service agencies, and management-training institutes.

Eighteen programs reported having advisory and/or steering committees comprising a variety of players, most of whom came from school districts; however, there was also representation from business, industry, and other community organizations. Several programs reported working with other universities or such national organizations as the National Association of Secondary School Principals. This is reminiscent of Pitner's call (1982) for collaborative efforts between and among school districts, professional associations, and universities.

School-district personnel played a variety of collaborative roles. Principals served as mentors, and both district-level officials and principals served on advisory committees. Practitioners assisted in program and curriculum development, taught courses or modules, attended such activities as reflective seminars and field trips, and helped in formulating program guidelines. Several programs reported that school-district personnel were instrumental in the recruitment and selection of candidates.

KEY STRENGTHS AND ISSUES

From their inception in the mid-1980s, the programs have been engaged in what some facilitators have called "stages of perpetual draft." That is, planning stages overlapped with implementation stages, which overlapped with planning stages, as programs continued to seek incremental improvements. Program evaluation was informal, continuous, and formative. Guidance was often provided by emerging research on such subjects as change in organizations, experiential learning, adult learning theory, internships, and mentoring. Still, workable models were imprecise, and facilitators often appeared to ground their programs in expedience and situational successes. Overall, program facilitators reported a number of productive programmatic initiatives in response to the survey's request for key strengths and key issues.

Key Strengths

Survey results suggest that program facilitators are optimistic about their programmatic innovations. They cited 56 program strengths and listed more strong points in the area of "departmental and university support for academic programming" than in any other. In addition, program facilitators perceived successes in such programmatic changes as the following:

- A more effectively integrated series of courses (University of Oklahoma)
- Modified course content and enrichment programming (University of Central Florida)
- Improved teaching and presenting; [having] every professor in the department [work] with the program (East Tennessee State)
- Modular format and presentations by practitioners (University of Alabama, University of Connecticut, and University of Tennessee)

- Field trips, especially to prisons and juvenile homes (City College of New York)
- Curriculum improvements; schedule and faculty changes (University of Washington)
- Curriculum and performance of faculty (University of Virginia)

Innovative curriculum changes were often described as "strong," "effective," or "creative and flexible," while the participation and support of departmental faculty were perceived as significant strengths.

As stated earlier, facilitators also viewed "cohorts" as a strength. Students in cohorts seem to be more motivated and of higher quality than those in earlier preparation programs. "To date," commented one facilitator, "scholars are developing into a highly motivated, collegial team." Others cited improved recruitment and screening methods that provide "exceptionally good students," "students as critical thinkers," "[high-]quality candidates," and excellent candidates "who might not otherwise participate."

Strengths, as perceived by facilitators, further included the enthusiasm of mentors, the efficacy of internship experiences, the connections with school districts, the productiveness of reflective seminars, and improvements in equity. Relative to improved equity, California State at Fresno described "an emphasis on experienced and ethnically diverse students," along with "attention to issues of ethnicity, poverty, and language in this region." City College of New York agreed and commented, "The program has already graduated 117 individuals during the past 2 years. It has been well-received throughout NYC and has had a positive impact on increasing administrative opportunities for minorities and females."

Key Issues

Programmatic strengths for some universities are challenges for others. According to survey data, the most mentioned category, "departmental and university support in academic programming," was viewed simultaneously among programs as both the strongest and the most problematic. Departmental support was mentioned by several programs as disappointing. In one case, the job of coordinating the program was made more difficult because of decreased "mobilization of educational administration program members." Other programs cited challenges in obtaining "department solidarity," "faculty support," "more involvement of faculty," or "real department commitment."

The typical university reward system was also cited as being nonsupportive of programs. One survey expressed its concern as follows:

> Faculty in major universities are rewarded with promotion and merit pay for research and publications, not for restructuring courses, advising students, supervising students in the field, designing and delivering special workshops that meet the perceived needs of students and field mentors. (University of Connecticut)

A small number of Danforth programs cited other issues. The following were troublesome areas for a few programs: cooperation of school districts, placement of interns with suitable mentors, release time for interns, the size of cohorts, and changing requirements in state certification standards. The differences among programs appeared to be related to such factors as the time since initiation of the program, the leadership of the program, the degree of specialization of faculty, and the commitment of faculty and administrators to principal preparation, among others.

Concluding Comments

Amid concerns surrounding the ways in which aspiring school administrators are prepared, there has been increasing agreement that changes are needed in university preparation programs. Since 1986, the Danforth Foundation has encouraged a number of university-preparation programs for school principals to initiate programs designed around field-based experiences and collaborative arrangements between universities and school districts. Twenty-two universities accepted the foundation's invitation to participate. In 1991, an effort to document the progress of DPPSP was undertaken.

Five years after the first Danforth interns enrolled, the program facilitators enthusiastically endorsed the power of field experiences in more effectively preparing novice administrators for positions of school leadership. They viewed mentoring principals as key players and school districts as valued partners in the preparation process. Program-delivery systems departed from traditional models, were grounded in adult learning theory, and tended to be field based. Program content remained rooted in the theoretical foundations of educational administration and fostered linkages with practice through reflective seminars and internships. Program facilitators attested to the power of the cohort in promoting cooperative learning, mutual support systems, and professional networking. Finally, program facilitators viewed their collaborative arrangements with school districts as indispensable sources of support and advocacy.

Have the participating universities established programs considerably different from their predecessors? Survey data suggest a positive response, especially regarding the importance of internship experiences, collaborating with school districts, the use of cohorts, and the value of mentoring relationships. Are Danforth programs more effective than previous programs in preparing school principals to meet the challenges of a practitioner's world? The study's descriptive data provided few evaluative answers. In 1991, Phase 2 of the DPPSP began. Arrangements to maintain baseline data throughout Phase 2 are already in place for future program evaluation. As the effort continues, the question of increased effectiveness invites systematic inquiry. For now, the chapters that follow, describing case studies of five Danforth programs, offer some early feedback about effectiveness.

References

Ashe, J., Haubner, J., & Troisi, N. (1991, September). University preparation of principals: The New York study. *NASSP Bulletin, 75*(536), 145-150.

Barnett, B. (1990). The mentor-intern relationship: Making the most of learning from experience. *NASSP Bulletin, 74,* 17-24.

Bova, B., & Phillips, R. (1984). Mentoring as a learning experience for adults. *Journal of Teacher Education, 35,* 16-20.

Carnegie Forum on Education and the Economy. (1986). *A nation prepared: Teachers for the 21st century.* New York: Carnegie Foundation.

Cordeiro, P., Krueger, J., Parks, D., Restine, L. N., & Wilson, P. (1992). *Taking stock: A survey of the Danforth programs for the preparation of school principals.* St. Louis, MO: The Danforth Foundation.

Daresh, J. (1988, April). *The role of mentors in preparing future leaders.* Paper presented at the annual meeting of the American Educational Research Association, New Orleans, LA.

Daresh, J., & Playko, M. (1989, April). *Reflections of a cycle I program.* Paper presented at the meeting of the Network of the Danforth Foundation Program for the Preparation of School Principals, Norman, OK.

Hills, J. (1975). The preparation of administrators: Some observations from the "firing line." *Educational Administration Quarterly, 11*(3), 1-20.

Hoyle, J. (1985). Programs in educational administration and the AASA preparation guidelines. *Educational Administrative Quarterly, 21*(1), 71-93.

Kram, K. (1985). Improving the mentoring process. *Training and Development Journal, 39,* 40-43.

Krueger, J. (1991). Clinical experiences in educational administration: A university collaborates with local school districts. *Journal of School Leadership, 1,* 252-265.

McCarthy, K., Kuh, G., & Beckman, J. (1979). Characteristics and attitudes of doctoral students in educational administration. *Phi Delta Kappan, 61*(3), 200-203.

McQuarrie, F. (1989, April). *The Oklahoma experience: The Danforth foundation principal preparation program.* Paper presented at the meeting of the Network for the Danforth Foundation for the Preparation of School Principals. Norman, OK.

Mueller, K., & Kendall, M. (1989, March). *Capturing leadership in action: Portraiture as a collaborative tool.* Paper presented at the meeting of the American Educational Research Association, San Francisco, CA.

National Association of Elementary School Principals. (1990). *Principals for 21st century schools.* Alexandria, VA: Author.

National Commission for Excellence in Educational Administration. (1987). *Leaders for tomorrow's schools.* Tempe, AZ: University Council for Educational Administration.

National Policy Board for Educational Administration. (1989). *Improving the preparation of school administrators: An agenda for reform.* Charlottesville: University of Virginia.

Papalewis, R., Jordan, M., Cuellar, A., Gaulden, J., & Smith, A. (1991, April). *Preparing school administrators for the culturally and linguis-*

tically diverse: A formal mentor training program in progress. Paper presented at the meeting of the American Educational Research Association, Chicago, IL.

Paulter, A. (1990). *A review of UCEA member institutions' clinical experiences/internships/field experiences for educational leaders.* Paper presented at the annual meeting of the University Council for Educational Administration, Pittsburgh, PA.

Pitner, N. J. (1982). *Training of the school administrator: State of the art* (occasional paper). Eugene, OR: Center for Educational Policy and Management.

Restine, L. N. (1990). *The evolution of meaning in an educational administration internship.* Unpublished doctoral dissertation, University of New Mexico, Albuquerque.

Ubben, G., & Fowler, F. (1989, October). *Strategies for organizing principal preparation: A survey of the Danforth principal preparation programs.* Paper presented at the annual meeting of the University Council for Educational Administration, Scottsdale, AZ.

University Council for Educational Administration. (1989). *The preparation of educational administrators: Statement of purpose adopted by the plenary session of the UCEA, October 27, 1989.* Tempe, AZ: Arizona State University.

There Must Be a Better Way

University of Alabama

The Administration and Educational Leadership Area of the University of Alabama's College of Education is one of the original members of the Danforth program. With its program in operation since 1987, its first 4 years have resulted in 67 Alabama Department of Education certified graduates. Presently finishing a fifth cohort, it will be expanding its intake to two new groups, one in Tuscaloosa and one in Gadsden, Alabama, during the coming summer.

Unlike institutions that joined the Danforth program in later cycles, the Alabama program had no prior role models to turn to for guidance in its program-change efforts. What it did have was a sense that there had to be a better way than the existing program, which was typical of offerings in higher-education institutions around the country. The press for leadership-preparation reform at the national level resulted in an intense interest to examine alternative approaches at the University of Alabama.

As the Danforth program that has continued the longest, the Leadership Area has demonstrated its ability to persevere and leave a lasting impact on the preparation of educational leaders throughout the state. The present chapter summarizes how this came about, as well as what is yet to be done. Contents include background information about the environment, the university, the Administration and Educational Leadership Area, and a description and analysis of the Danforth program.

Setting

The University of Alabama's oldest campus, founded in 1831, is in Tuscaloosa, Alabama, a city of about 80,000 people in west-central Alabama, which is about 60 miles southwest of Birmingham. The university has become a comprehensive center of higher education, housing 14 schools and colleges with nearly 150 academic areas and more than 300 accredited undergraduate and graduate degree programs, which enroll more than 19,000 students, about 2,500 of whom are graduate students.

The university places a high priority on its efforts to positively impact the state's public schools. In fact, according to a university report, as early as 1913, the president of the university described the institution as the "crowning achievement of Alabama's public school system. The University's work . . . rests upon the public elementary schools." Teaching cannot be fragmented by age and grade: "Kindergarten through doctoral study is a seamless web of learning." The current dean of the College of Education feels that this commitment, which is rather distinctive among universities, is still true today. The College of Education, which is composed of six subject areas, houses about 93 full-time and 19 part-time faculty who oversee the education of about 1,650 undergraduate students (1,335 are full time) and 541 graduate students (184 are full time).

The Administration and Educational Leadership Area houses three programs: Administration and Planning, Administration and Instructional Leadership, and Higher Education. The faculty, evenly distributed among these programs, consists of 9 full-time faculty members and the Area head, four of whom, including the Area head, have joined the program within the past 3 years. There are also a number of other professors who teach part time in the Area, including the associate dean and an assistant dean.

The Area provides programs for the basic certification level, advanced certification/education-specialist level, master's, Ed.D., and Ph.D. degrees in each of its three programs. It serves the preparation needs of educators from across the entire state and, for that matter, of educators from neighboring states who avail themselves of the Area's services. About 65% of the Area's students come from outside the immediate Tuscaloosa metropolitan area. These students represent the state's rural, urban, and suburban communities.

The Area's students are diverse, with different experiential backgrounds and career goals. Those in the Higher Education Program are preparing for administrative positions in colleges and universities. Those in the Administration and Planning Program are preparing for elementary, secondary, and central office administration. Those in the Administration and Instructional Leadership Program are preparing for supervisory, human resource management, and staff-development positions, in settings as diverse as nursing preparation and public management, as well as in more traditional precollegiate institutions.

Prior to initiation of the Danforth program, the Area focused much of its preparation efforts toward the advanced certification/Ed.S. level (the state's department of education requires administrators to return for further graduate training within 5 years of taking their first administrative position) and toward the doctoral level. There are not many candidates for the Area's master's degree, because the state department requires that school districts can only claim master's-level reimbursement for teachers who earn the M.A. in their teaching-preparation area. This significantly reduces the press for master's-level preparation in administration.

Readiness for Change

The Danforth program at the University of Alabama represents a significant shift from the traditional program, which is cafeteria-style in approach. Readiness for change came from several sources. First, the dean of the College of Education was interested in promoting a different approach to the preparation of educational leaders. Having chaired an educational administration program elsewhere, he felt

that the approach taken at that institution, as well as by other programs with which he was familiar, left much to be desired. He was
also specifically concerned about preparation in Alabama because of
projections that indicated a 50% turnover among school administrators in 3 to 5 years.

In response to these concerns, he took several actions. First,
believing that major changes would have to be undertaken, he proposed to the 1984 Governor's Commission on Education that the M.A.
should be a degree taken in one's area of initial preparation. The
Commission supported this position. This led to a State Board of
Education change that made entry-level certification as an administrator contingent on prior completion of an M.A. degree in one's
teaching area. This left university-based preparation programs to
focus on administrative certification only. Second, he contacted the
Danforth Foundation to see whether it could provide resources for
the Area as it developed effective responses to the state's changes.
Third, once the Area developed its new program, the dean, as a
member of the 1988 State Board of Education Task Force that was
charged with reviewing preparation programs, was able to get the
University of Alabama's program format accepted as the new approach to certification for all of the 28 institutions preparing administrators in Alabama.

The dean's actions were accompanied by actions in the Area,
which recognized that the state's certification changes were rapidly
leading to lost appeal for its master's degree. It would have to develop
an effective response, or its efforts would be skewed toward the
doctorate and toward advanced preparation at the Ed.S. level. Thus
responding to the press by the dean, the changing rules of the state's
department of education, and the general ferment in the field of
preparation during the mid-1980s, the Area made an effort to rethink
its response to the changing needs of entry-level school administrators.

The faculty asked the long-term Area head, who was stepping
down from this post, to guide them through a reexamination of
entry-level preparation activities. His prior experience as a principal
and superintendent and his knowledge of the preparation field made
him ideally suited to pursue this activity. Under his guidance, the
faculty began a series of discussions to clarify the purposes of an
entry-level preparation program. With little by way of an established,

in-place program, and thus with little need to be weaned away from an ingrained approach, faculty members were open to looking at new options. The faculty ultimately agreed that a new program should be designed and implemented, which would emphasize entry-level skills to, as they put it, "survive" the first years in the principalship. When the Danforth Foundation invited the Area to apply for a grant to implement their ideas and become a member of the foundation's first cycle, the faculty was ready to accept the challenge.

Description of the Program

To identify required leadership skills, the faculty had graduate students do a review of the literature. They identified approximately 200 skills necessary for surviving the principalship. These were submitted for review by advisory committees of principals, who pared the number to 81. These skills, with subsequent modifications, became the basis of the Area's curriculum at the initial level of certification.

Regarding the clinical part of the program, initially, an understanding was reached between the Area personnel and the local superintendents that would give students much more time-on-task, including extended opportunities during the school day to shadow and work with their administrators. Specifically, it was agreed that students would qualify for an unpaid semester leave of absence, during which time they would participate in course work on campus. They would also have a semester in a full-time role as an intern working with a site administrator. It soon became apparent that students felt that they could not afford an unpaid leave of a semester's duration. In addition, superintendents were pressured by their staff members, and often by teacher union officials, to back away from seeking funding for paid internships because this might be viewed as favoring one group of teachers' professional development objectives over those of others.

Given these limitations, the Area reexamined its proposed framework and developed a design for curriculum and internship activities that it hoped would serve the basic intent. The program coordinator also negotiated an understanding with the state's department of education to protect the Area's certification applicants. The state department's response was to permit testing of the new program for several years, while assuring the Area's graduates that they would be granted certification upon completion.

ACADEMIC CONTENT AND DELIVERY

There are three key aspects of the academic content and delivery. First, the academic content is packaged as modules, most of which are presented in 2-hour blocks. Modules are based on skills and knowledge required in the principalship: the structure of American public schools, leadership styles, word processing, curriculum sequencing, evaluation of classroom performance, clinical supervision, staff development, computer applications, due process for students, personnel documentation, time management, stress management, decision making, support staff management, and administration of testing programs. Originally designed around "survival skills," the content of modules is being expanded to include a more balanced emphasis on instructional leadership skills such as curriculum change and program and teacher evaluation, as well as on building management skills. The modules are taught over a 10-week period in the summer prior to the year in which students do their internships. Students take these modules together in a cohort of 20.

Second, those responsible for preparing and teaching the modules include full-time faculty members, faculty members from across the campus (e.g., stress management is taught by a faculty member from the Psychology Department, and communication skills are taught by a professor from the Communications Department), and by leading practitioners, including area superintendents and the state superintendent, who have special knowledge about specific skill areas. Approximately 50% of the modules are taught by such practitioners. The mix of module presenters ensures that students receive interdisciplinary perspectives and insights from practitioners who practice what they teach, as well as the insights and thinking of Area faculty members.

To enhance instruction, instructors submit a module plan as well as readings and module objectives for student review prior to the time of presentations. Equally important, team teaching is done with some regularity, teaming Area faculty members with practitioners, as well as with faculty members from other units in the university. In addition, there are "integrating" seminars every 2 weeks, to bring the module content to a higher level of comprehension. Plans are under way to make integration a daily activity.

Third, students are asked each day during the summer to evaluate modules and the individuals teaching them. Also, an annual evaluation is conducted of both the campus-based and field-site components of the program. As a result of these evaluations, which are conducted by doctoral students in the Area, a number of changes have been made in the modules being presented, the individuals called on to present them, and the partnerships and mentoring activities that take place in the field. A new "bridging" class is also planned for the incoming cohorts, which will bring students on campus for 2 weeks in each of the fall and spring semesters. This should help to maintain and build on learnings gained during the intensive summer experience. Finally, the faculty has begun a practice of inviting all program graduates to join them on campus two times a year to review and rethink the program's curriculum.

STUDENTS

Students in the University of Alabama's Danforth program must meet several admissions criteria. First, they must be recommended by their school district's superintendent or their principal, who will serve as the supervisor if they are admitted to the program. Students must also possess a master's degree in a teaching field and must develop a file, which includes their transcripts. They must additionally complete a written essay on educational leadership issues.

On an annual basis, the number of applicants is about 100, with the maximum number of students admitted to a cohort being limited to 20. During the first 4 years, the Area served 67 students, and a current group of 20 is completing its program. For the sixth year, the Area is admitting two cohort groups, one in Tuscaloosa and one in Gadsden, which is 2 hours to the northeast of the university. Thus the intake will increase from a maximum of 20 to a maximum of 40.

Applicants come from across the state, as well as from neighboring states. The mix of applicants is fairly representative of the state's rural/suburban/urban population composition. On average, about 35% of those admitted are from the Tuscaloosa metropolitan area.

The male-to-female ratio has averaged 22% to 78%, and the African-/European-American ratio has averaged 25% to 75%. This racial mix, which is about the same as the racial mix for the traditional program, is substantially above that of the overall 6% African-American student population at the University of Alabama. However, as compared to the racial mix in the city's schools, which is about 60% African-American in the student group and 40% African-American in the teacher group, the Area may have to increase its recruitment of this minority group to increase the pool of racial-minority leadership talent.

Given the prior achievement of an M.A., most students (88%) are taking nondegree, certification work in the Area. It should be noted that a few applicants hold provisional certification and are already in administrative positions.

Advisement of Danforth program students is done by the co-hort's coordinator. This practice ensures that students receive guidance that is directly related to progressing through their programs.

The Area has not maintained records of its graduates' success in obtaining administrative positions. However, subjective judgment indicates that they are gaining employment at an impressive rate. Perhaps as many as 70% of those who seek administrative positions obtain them. The faculty hears from its graduates, many of whom report active employment as administrators. The faculty also maintains close ties with school system leaders, who report that they prefer hiring Danforth Program graduates over other applicants being trained in the state. In fact, one superintendent told the faculty that he intends to limit his selection pool to graduates of this program.

INTERNSHIP

There are four key aspects of the internship program. First, the Area Coordinator requires students to have at least 500 hours of site-based clinical activities, which is 200 hours above the state's department of education certification requirements and the number of hours the traditional program's students are expected to fulfill. According to state certification requirements passed in January of

1992, interns must divide 300 clinical hours as follows: 50 in an elementary school, 50 in a middle/junior high school, 50 in a high school, 50 in a central office, and the remaining 100 in whichever area of preparation is their special interest. This now requires that the Area and school districts develop ways of ensuring that students obtain these diverse experiences. Site supervisors, who are referred to as "mentors," are normally principals at the students' schools.

Second, the Area provides students and mentors with a manual describing activities to be covered. These activities are quite specific, and include such subjects as maintenance, budgeting, and physical plant, as well as instructional leadership and facilitation of change. After reviewing the manual, a contract is developed so that all parties are clear about expectations. Currently, the manual is being modified to reflect learnings gleaned over the past 5 years, and to reflect the decision to provide more emphasis on instructional leadership.

Third, the time available for internship activities during the school day is severely limited. Students typically are employed full-time with teaching duties or an equivalent set of expectations. To at least partially compensate for this limitation, interns are expected to work with their mentors the week before school opens in the fall and the week after it closes for the summer.

Beyond this common expectation, time-on-task and quality of experiences vary greatly, depending on the mentors' degree of commitment, ability, and willingness to release the intern from other duties; the kinds of activities in which they involve the interns; and the quality of mentoring they are able to give interns.

Fourth, the interns return to campus four times each year for a full day on Saturdays, to share their experiences, meet with faculty, and receive further enrichment experiences, such as learning how to apply for an administrative position. Interns also provide feedback, which is used by the faculty for program improvements.

As noted, the original intent was to have students experience a semester-long, full-time internship. Unfortunately, lack of resources, as well as limiting political dynamics, made it impossible to pursue this plan. As a result, the internship has not been of the intensity that planners intended. Students currently must still fulfill regular employment duties as classroom teachers or other professionals.

This has created a major problem: How will students have the opportunity to fulfill internship expectations? The Area and participating school administrators are trying to find ways of responding to these limitations. As noted, the Area requires students to report a full week before school begins, remain on site for a week after school is over, and work with supervising administrators during holidays when these individuals are required to be in the building. The faculty also requires interns to participate in related activities, such as preparing and delivering staff-development workshops and observing school-board meetings. A new activity that will be implemented during the coming academic year is the bridging class noted earlier, which will bring interns together on campus for extended periods of time to diagnose, analyze, and synthesize site-based situations.

For their part, some administrators are seeking ways of relieving students of nonessential responsibilities to extend their time for internship experiences. If they can obtain resources to provide a substitute to cover the intern's classroom, mentors have the intern take over the building when they must be away.

However, these measures are not sufficient to fulfill the minimum internship hours expectation. As a result, interns have to find time prior to the school day, during their planning periods, and after the school day. This makeshift response, which is in addition to regular professional-duty expectations, can be exhausting. More important, it falls short of the intended quality of the internship experience. It becomes quite difficult to be introduced to, let alone to master, administrative role responsibilities when time-on-task is limited and sporadic, rather than extensive and regularized.

Under such conditions, the quality of the internship experience becomes more problematic. Extraordinary efforts on the part of the faculty, district leaders, and school-site supervisors are called for. For their part, as noted, the faculty has tried to be supportive by having interns return to campus a full day twice per semester to review and analyze field-site experiences. This will be expanded to 2 days twice each semester, starting with the incoming cohort. What is also required is a greater presence of faculty, as field supervisors, at school sites. This would lend support to the students' efforts to get more time-on-task for internship work. At present, according to new Alabama Department of Education rules, faculty members are charged with responsibility for intern supervision. However, most visit sites only a few times a year.

Superintendents have felt constrained financially and politically, fearing the perception that they are showing favoritism if they provide extended opportunities for internship time during the day for potential administrators, while not providing equal time for other teachers. Site supervisors, as might be expected, differ in their responses. Some have tried to release interns from other duties, provide occasional substitutes, get district permission to establish temporary administrative roles, and in any way possible, lavish time and creative energy on their interns. Others have not taken such initiative.

In such circumstances, the quality of the internship experience that students receive becomes a matter of chance. This has been a major problem for many preparation programs across the country, and it is an important issue that must be addressed by universities, school districts, state education departments, state legislatures, and governors.

COORDINATION

One of the Area's faculty members is charged with coordination of the Danforth program. The first and second coordinators were tenured senior faculty members with longtime service at the university. The first coordinator, who had been Area head prior to taking on this role, remained with the program for 2 years before retiring. The second coordinator is finishing his third cycle of Danforth program students and will step down from this activity at the end of the academic year. For the coming year, there will be two coordinators, one for the ongoing Tuscaloosa-based program and the other to start up a cohort at the university's northern outreach branch at Gadsden. The incoming coordinators are relatively new to the Area and are not yet well known by the state's school-district leadership group. Their involvement is leading to implementation of modifications such as new modules and more contacts with cohort groups on campus during the academic year. However, it is possible that their lack of recognition by school leaders may make it more difficult, at least at the outset, to develop effective partnerships.

FINANCIAL ARRANGEMENTS

The Area has creatively developed a financial base to promote excellence in the academic program. First, it used Danforth's unrestricted funds to develop further its partnership with regional superintendents and principals by, for example, sponsoring meetings, holding luncheons, and paying travel expenses for program-related activities. Second, it developed a unique arrangement with the university, by which students pay their tuition to the College of Continuing Studies, and their payments are remitted to the Area to be used for program development and operation purposes. For example, professors from across campus, as well as practitioner-leaders from school districts, are paid small honorariums to teach modules. Third, the Area requires students to pay a $100 materials fee to support duplication and dissemination of materials. Together, these various resource-gathering strategies enable the Area to maintain a program that is widely recognized for its quality, practicality, and relevance.

Unfortunately, funding for internship release time is not yet available. While the state mandates an internship, no resources have been made available to support it. Similarly, local school districts are unable to provide such resources because they have been under fiscal duress, particularly over the past few years, as the state's budget for education has been reduced. The outcome is that students are unable to obtain the rich field experiences needed to apply skills learned in the academic program.

Analysis

The University of Alabama's Danforth program has been in operation for almost 5 years. The Area has, in fact, decided to drop the traditional program and require all candidates seeking entry-level certification to do so through the Danforth approach. Further, as an indicator of the positive value placed on the program, the state's department of education has recently mandated that, with minor modifications, the model developed by the Area will be the certification program that all preparation institutions in Alabama must follow.

BENEFICIAL PAYOFFS

Payoffs for Students

Several advantages are perceived by students who go through the program. Many note that the Area's faculty is highly qualified, has a strong administrative experiential base, and is genuinely caring and concerned about its students and the school districts. Supportive of this perception is the Area's consensus decision that all faculty members will donate 4 days of free consulting to school districts each year.

Present and former students feel that the academic program is needed by those entering administration, particularly because it is intensive and focused within a 12-month period of time. More important, the emphasis on basic skills such as communications, conflict management, strategic and tactical planning, administrative and instructional applications of computers, supervision, discipline, and plant management can be put to immediate use in administrative positions. Further, in addition to presentations by Area faculty members, program content is delivered by leading practitioners who are experts in the module areas they teach, as well as by faculty members who come from a variety of behavioral science orientations across the campus. This approach, which has proven to be a rich one for students, is worthy of review by other preparation programs.

Students place great value on going through the program in cohorts. During the intensive 10 weeks of the summer academic program, members help one another cope with the massive amount of new information. During the year, they come together four times on campus, renewing group interactions as they explore learnings from internship experiences. After the program, many maintain close relationships, helping each other overcome initial entry-level problems, providing opportunities to process feelings and issues, and even helping to identify available positions.

Finally, although hard data are not available, it does appear that program graduates are being hired in large numbers. Feedback from those who have found administrative positions indicates that they feel well prepared to confront management problems with confidence.

Payoffs for Site Supervisors

Payoffs for site supervisors, beyond the $100 honorarium they get for coming to campus for a half-day training session, are mixed. First, for many, involvement as a site supervisor is not necessarily a purposeful decision. Rather, it is a matter of being the principal at a school in which a student in the preparation program is a teacher. Second, although there is some preparation for playing the role, that preparation is limited to a half-day of activities at the university during the summer session. Third, due to financial constraints already identified, there is little time available during the day to work with interns, so the full potential for mentoring and professional growth that such interactions offer is not easy to obtain. Fourth, the management assistance that site supervisors get from interns is constrained because of the limited amount of time available during the school day.

Payoffs for School Districts

The superintendent of the Tuscaloosa City Schools noted, "The Danforth program is a godsend for us. We are able to locate administrators and promote change in the profession. We get the right individuals who have the right skills. Graduates of the program are different—they have a better range, more contacts, more skills and knowledge, are current on problems we face, and very practical in their approach. It is, in effect, a feeder system for the district." Other administrators also recognize the value of the program to their districts. For example, a county superintendent noted that his three top administrators are Danforth graduates.

School leaders also benefit from the opportunities for professional development as a result of their participation in the program. For example, many serve on Area advisory committees, teach modules in the program, and supervise interns.

Despite the recognized advantages of the program, many school leaders are still cautious about the support they will give to the effort. In particular, they hesitate to refuse requests for recommendations by candidates who they do not support, fearing accusations of discrimination, as well as the potential for grievances, negative teachers union reactions, and even legal challenges. Neither have they sought creative ways of finding on-task time for interns who are not funded for these activities.

Despite these difficulties, program graduates who have obtained administrative positions are beginning to have an impact on Alabama's school systems. Further, they are also nominating other excellent candidates for the Area's program, acting as mentors, and teaching modules in the program.

Payoffs for the University/College of Education/Area

Institutionalization of the program supports the university's stated priority of serving the needs of the state's elementary and secondary school student population. Over time, the university has been supportive of this goal and, in the present instance, has shown this support by allowing the Area to experiment with a novel approach to the delivery of its curriculum and by allowing the unit to use tuition monies to support that program.

The College of Education has also benefited from the development of the new program. As partnering and networking increase, the college's image as caring and supportive of the state's school systems is enhanced. Given that there are many institutions of higher education preparing educators in the state, and that the university, as a research institute, is not always viewed as responsive to local school-district needs, this is an important outcome.

The Area has benefited from the program change in a number of ways:

1. Credibility with the state's department of education, which, as noted, has adopted the Danforth program model with some modifications for certification requirements, is quite high. The state superintendent even teaches in the program.
2. Through regular evaluation efforts and feedback from students and others, the Area has been able to modify and improve its academic program. This summer, it will offer the Danforth program as the only entry-level preparation program.

3. The modular approach promotes the likelihood that the Area will remain current in its academic offerings, because it is much easier to add and remove modules than it is to add and remove courses. In fact, as a result of feedback and changing environmental conditions, a number of modules have been modified or dropped and new ones have been added since the inception of the program. For example, site-based management is a growing reality and is therefore being given focused academic time as a module.

4. More important, the Area has been very responsive to the changing role of the building administrator and has added academic experiences that emphasize instructional leadership. Even courses are undergoing change. For example, 6 hours of the 45 hours required for courses are now expected to be a field experience for students in the advanced administrative certification program.

5. As the Area focuses on program development at the more advanced Ed.S. and doctorate levels, it is building on the learnings gained in the Danforth program. Both the Ed.S. and the doctoral program will enroll students in cohort groups, provide intensive academic experiences, and require some form of internship activities. There is even evidence of an extended spill-over effect on an Area international-preparation outreach effort that involves off-site instruction and the awarding of the M.A. to administrators of English-speaking schools in a number of Latin American settings. This program effort is being redesigned to include learnings gained in the Danforth program, such as focus on skills and enrollment of cohort groups.

6. There is also a staff-development program being prepared for English-speaking educators in 35 Latin American countries, which is benefiting from the skill-based, modular approach designed for the Danforth program. These spill-over effects may ultimately be as important to the effectiveness of the Area's preparation efforts as the advantages gained by the changes established at the entry level.

7. Faculty in the Area, including senior faculty, as well as those who joined the Area over the past few years, support the new initiative. The orientation toward entry-level training and the Alabama Department of Education's new certification rules require full-time faculty members to serve as interns' field supervisors, so they are spending an increasing amount of time in schools. This is likely to have a positive impact in several ways: enrichment of faculty teaching efforts, increased faculty recognition by educational leaders (which is particularly important for those new to the state), opportunities for cooperative efforts with school-district leaders as a result of expanded networking, and a rich source of data for research and writing. A renewed desire for professional development is present among faculty members, at least partly as a result of their involvement as field supervisors and module presenters in the program.

8. Practitioners who have taught modules are becoming more supportive of the program. Their firsthand involvement is making it clear to them that the Area has developed a strong and meaningful response to the leadership needs of school districts. This reservoir of goodwill is certainly beneficial to the Area.

ONGOING ISSUES

The Administration and Educational Leadership Area has made major strides toward the creation and maintenance of a unique and effective response to the educational leadership needs of the state's school systems. The achievements are real and meaningful. However, as the Area head noted, "We are still in our infancy and there is much to be done."

Academic Program

The presentation of skills and knowledge in a 10-week period during the initial summer of the program helps shift students' perceptions from those of teachers to those of administrators. It also promotes the understanding of the parts as they come together to form a whole regarding required administrator survival skills and knowledge. However, as program graduates have noted, there is little opportunity to practice and incorporate these learnings because academic content is delivered prior to the commencement of the internship. Further, as already noted, the internship may not provide sufficient time-on-task to practice these learnings.

Regarding content of the program, the original focus on the principal as manager is recognized as being in need of change. Efforts are already under way to enhance the extent of content that focuses on instructional leadership, in part due to the Alabama Department of Education's change to a single certificate for all supervisors and administrators, and in part due to the faculty's recognition of the changing definition of the school administrator's role to facilitator of instructional change. The curriculum will thus change from a predominant focus on building management to one that will devote about 50% of module presentation time to educational leadership skills and knowledge.

Similarly, the focus should be broadened to encompass the unique role requirements of the assistant principal. Most program graduates move into this position for at least some period of time. They would benefit greatly from some added skill and knowledge focused on topics such as student discipline.

The Area does an excellent job of evaluating curricular offerings and of making improvements based on these evaluations. However, it would also be beneficial for instructors to receive the results of these evaluations, particularly if they are asked back to make future presentations.

Recruitment and Admissions

The Area has been purposefully attempting to increase the quality of its entry-level student group. In pursuit of this objective, it has established a principal and superintendent sponsorship system to identify individuals with the potential to move into administrative positions.

There are still problems to be overcome. Efforts toward purposeful recruitment, perhaps asking teachers as well as administrators to make nominations, could further enhance the composition and quality of the pool of applicants. It is also desirable to increase the pool of racial- and ethnic-minority applicants from the current 25% to something closer to the 40% or more minority group that is in teaching positions in many of the state's school districts. The fact that the Area, with the Alabama LEAD Center as a partner, last year sponsored an all-day workshop for racial and ethnic minorities and women to recruit candidates from these groups, indicates that it is fully aware of the problem.

At the admissions level, the basis for judgment is currently limited to academic criteria such as transcripts, recommendations, and written essays. Given the intention of training those with leadership potential, it may be helpful to consider an expanded set of criteria and measurements that promote this end. For example, evidence of leadership-related experience such as chairing a curriculum committee, might be requested, and an assessment center might be used. The Area recognizes this need and is now exploring the possibility of instituting an assessment center as one source of judgment about admissions.

Finally, given principals' and superintendents' stated concerns about discriminating among teachers when recommendations are requested, instituting a practitioner/university screening committee for final admissions decisions might be helpful. Such a committee could make these critically important selection decisions in a confidential and effective manner, particularly if admissions folders include the aforementioned expanded evidence.

Internships

This is the element that is acknowledged by everyone—superintendents, principals and students, as well as faculty members—as the weakest link in the program. The constraints, as noted throughout this report, are numerous but not insurmountable. Responses that might be considered to impact these negative realities include the following:

1. The faculty can work with superintendents to be more selective in the identification and nomination of mentors because

these role players have the most important influence, positive or negative, on the intern. District leaders might consider providing mentors with written guidelines for this activity. The faculty can expand on the socialization and training time provided for mentors. Also, some interns may have to be moved to other school sites to conduct their internships. There are many precedents around the nation for this course of action.

2. Faculty members who serve as field supervisors may need to consider being present in the school sites on a more regular basis. Partly, this is so that they can be more aware of and responsive to interns' growth needs, and partly, it is so that they can help socialize site supervisors to their role requirements.

3. All parties involved need to pool their creative energies to find ways around the limitations placed on interns regarding time-on-task. For example, summer school internship opportunities can be explored, and release time, even if some financial contribution on the part of the intern is required, can be examined.

The Area's Danforth program requires 500 internship hours of its students. Unless creative ways are found to promote high-quality experiences at least at this level of involvement, it probably will only be a short time before the program reverts to the 300 hours required by the state's department of education. The average time-on-task of Danforth programs around the country is closer to 600 hours, so it is important that the Area and school leaders seek ways of retaining and strengthening the number of hours that interns encounter in their field experiences.

Placement

A belief exists among faculty members and district leaders that graduates of the program are finding administrative positions at a much greater rate than those who complete the traditional program, or those who go through programs at the other 27 Alabama institutions providing preparation programs for educational leadership.

However, there are no hard data to substantiate these beliefs. It would be meaningful to find out whether the current belief system is supported by the facts.

Financing

The academic program and its delivery system have a strong and secure financial base, but resources needed to support sufficient time to learn the realities of the job during the school day are woefully inadequate. This problem is widely recognized, but there is little active exploration to seek ways to overcome the problem. Given the state's department of education requirement of 300 hours of internship, activities aimed at seeking state-level funding for this activity may be both appropriate and important. It would probably not lead to immediate payoffs, but such pressure might have positive results in the long run. If nothing else, bringing interested parties together might lead to innovative and creative solutions beyond that of state-level funding. For example, such possibilities as commitment of local support, reserving one or more administrative positions on a revolving basis for intern activities, or agreeing on realistic ways to promote release time might be explored.

Partnering

The Area wisely called on superintendent and principal committees to help clarify purposes and curriculum content when it implemented the new program. However, regular attention to these partnerships has not been pursued vigorously. Because there is some way to go before the full potential of the program's purposes is fulfilled, reenergizing the partnership and ensuring that it will continue to function are important activities to pursue. Many and varied ideas can be gained and support that can be achieved through such arrangements (e.g., improvement of recruitment and selection of participants; maintaining curriculum at the cutting edge of knowledge and skill needs; and more effective responses to current internship limitations). The Area may want to explore the possibility of creating a representative group of superintendents and principals to meet regularly with Area faculty members to provide such feedback.

Coordination

The transition of program leadership means that four different faculty members have been involved in coordination activities between the summer of 1987 and the summer of 1992. The Area was able to make the first leadership transition smoothly, in part because of the dedication, networking capabilities, senior faculty status, and reputations of the first two coordinators. Dedication is also a mark of the incoming co-coordinators, both of whom have already been meeting with their first cohorts, 3 months before these groups begin the program.

Besides promoting wider faculty involvement and support, leadership transitions have the advantage of bringing new perspectives to the program. For example, the co-coordinators are introducing new structural elements and curricular content.

However, there may also be disadvantages. Unless there is full and open communication between outgoing and incoming coordinators, the norms and expectations, as well as the learnings gained, may be jeopardized. If, as in the present case, those assigned to the program coordination activity are relatively new to the state, they will not have extensive networks with district leaders. This can make it more difficult to manage field aspects of the program. If this does happen, the coordinators will need faculty support in understanding the history and intent of the program, as well as help in establishing effective connections with school-district leaders.

In Alabama, the transition has been made smoother because the state's department of education has mandated, with a few modifications, the program's design as the requirement for administrator certification. The program is, in other words, the new certification model, so everyone—coordinators, faculty and school-district leaders alike—will be guided and constrained by the need to prepare the Area's students to fulfill these requirements.

A separate but important coordinator-related issue has to do with tenure. If, as in the case with the University of Alabama's incoming co-coordinators, faculty members are on the tenure track but have not yet achieved this goal, they will need the faculty's counseling and support. Without it, they will have difficulty achieving tenure while meeting the heavy service responsibilities associated with coordination of the program.

In Closing

With the institutionalization of its new program, the University of Alabama has now come full course toward a reconceptualization of purposes and a major reorientation in the operationalization of its educational leadership preparation program. Challenges remain, as the faculty expands its geographical scope and major shifts in leadership continue. However, institutionalization has clearly been accomplished, and a return to the old program design is unlikely. The accomplishment is all the more impressive, given that the University of Alabama was one of the original Danforth sites and, as such, there was little precedent to guide the effort.

From a Minimal Program
to the Renaissance

University of Central Florida

The University of Central Florida is a member of the fifth cycle of Danforth programs. Beginning its activities in the summer of 1990, the Educational Leadership Program already has 19 graduates. Another 20 students are finishing the program, and 20 to 25 more enrolled for the 1992 fall semester. Thus in just 2 years, a large number of educators have been attracted to participate in a challenging and comprehensive preparation program for educational leadership positions, a program the faculty continues to examine and modify as experience accumulates and environmental conditions change.

The arrival of a new graduate coordinator who was interested in exploring more effective ways of preparing educational leaders created the impetus for change. Fortunately, the faculty was not highly committed to the status quo offerings. In fact, because they did not view what they were doing as a serious programmatic approach to preparation, they were quite willing to explore alternative approaches.

The Setting

There are already 1.7 million people in the central Florida area, one of the fastest-growing regions in the United States. School districts are experiencing up to 12% annual growth rates, with the Hispanic-American community growth rate being most pronounced and rapidly changing the ethnic composition of many schools in the area. The biggest district, Orange County Public Schools (metropolitan Orlando), is the 20th largest in the United States, with more than 123,000 students, 7,000 teachers, 6,000 classified staff members, and 625 administrators. Forty-seven languages are spoken by the district's student population, the mix of which is 60% European-American, 26% African-American, 11% Hispanic-American, with the rest being Asian-American or Native American.

Although enrollments are increasing, financial support is decreasing. For example, the Orange County School District is growing by approximately 5,000 students annually, but budget cuts may force a reduction of up to 600 staff members.

The only public comprehensive higher education institution in central Florida opened the doors of its one building to 1,200 undergraduate students in 1968 as the Florida Technological University, then changed its name to the University of Central Florida in 1978. The College of Education had only 13 faculty members. Today, the 50-building university is a comprehensive institution with a special mission to promote the economic and technological development of the central Florida region. There are approximately 22,000 students, 3,200 of whom major in the College of Education, which houses 60 full-time faculty members.

The Educational Leadership Program, with 4 full-time and 6 part-time faculty members, is the largest of five units in the Educational Services Department. The others are Counseling, School Psychology, Institutional Technologies, and Media. The Leadership Program has approximately 200 graduate-level students, most of whom attend on a part time basis—130 at the master's/certification level and 70 at the doctoral level. A few faculty members have been at the university for more than 20 years, but most have arrived since 1985. The current and incoming internship coordinators are in their second and first years, respectively, as faculty members.

Most of the Leadership Program's student clientele comes from central Florida school districts, which are organized by counties. These districts differ in size, growth rates, and ethnic composition, as well as along an urban, suburban, and rural continuum. The area the Leadership Program serves extends about 60 miles east to west and 60 miles north to south.

Readiness for Change

During the 1980s, responding to calls for reform, both nationally and in Florida, the state's department of education examined what it felt to be essential requirements for effective education. Studies that were commissioned documented the relationship between effective schools and effective leadership. Competencies were identified that differentiated incompetent, competent, and excellent leaders.

The conclusion drawn was that many of the state's school administrators did not exhibit the qualities attributed to excellent leaders. Not surprisingly, the state's universities were assigned some of the blame for this situation.

Despite this negative conclusion, the department of education's certification requirements put minimal pressure on universities to change. Entry-level certification ("Level I"), which is applicable to any administrative position in elementary and secondary education, requires that candidates have a master's degree in any area, including educational administration (called "educational leadership" in Florida) and take an educational administration academic program. The specific number of hours varies across the nine state universities, from a low of 6 to a high of 10, with the norm being 7 or 8. Two courses in curriculum are also required, but there is no requirement for an internship.

After its plan was reviewed and a site visit was conducted in 1989, the University of Central Florida became the first program approved by the state's department of education.

State certification requirements do not appear to challenge the state's universities to provide practitioner-oriented programs. However, after completing their preparation programs, candidates for certification must pass a state examination, which thus allows the department to maintain a quality check on universities. Interestingly, the examination is written by a committee that is composed of roughly three university faculty members for every school-district administrator.

Rather than trying to significantly change the universities, the state's department of education instituted a "Level II" requirement. With Level I certification attained, candidates are permitted to seek administrative employment. Once they find a position, the hiring district becomes responsible for providing newly hired administrators with training and supervision for 2 years (during this time, new administrators must work in at least two different positions and with two different supervisors) and for collecting evidence of sufficiency on state-generated leadership competencies. For example, Orange County's Level II curriculum provides training that includes clarification of leadership styles, exploration of facilitation and problem-solving skills, writing development plans, and receiving feedback. If candidates successfully complete this process, the state's department of education grants them their permanent administrative license.

Given these conditions—the state's department of education's negative attitude about the role of higher education in training school leaders and the absence of challenging preservice certification rules—the Leadership Program could have continued unchanged. Instead, much to their credit, the faculty at the University of Central Florida viewed the situation as a challenge and responded in a proactive manner.

Until the mid-1980s, the Leadership Program offered students a traditional, behavioral sciences oriented, preparation program. Students at the master's/certification level selected courses such as finance, law, and theory, according to their own time availability. Until 1988, a thesis served as a culminating experience. In fact, although the internship was an option to the thesis, it was not promoted by the faculty. Few students opted for it, and the faculty provided little supervision or direction for those who did chose to do an internship.

In 1985, the Educational Services Department's newly arrived Director of Doctoral Programs, who is a member of the Educational Leadership Program, encouraged the faculty to examine its curriculum offerings. The major focus of the effort was the doctoral program, which was redesigned over the next 2 years, but thought was also given to the entry-level program. The director was concerned that the program did not appear to have an overall framework and, most important, it did not encompass a meaningful internship experience. Although the internship was an option to the thesis, students were not encouraged to take this clinical experience.

It is interesting to note that faculty members did not resist the review and changes. This was due to two factors. First, they did not feel committed to the program as it then existed because they thought it was not particularly strong. Second, as part of their university roles, most were administering other activities. They were pleased that someone else was taking the initiative because they were heavily preoccupied with other duties.

In the 1987-1988 academic year, after the doctoral program changes were in place, the faculty turned its full attention to the master's program. As a result of this review, they agreed to encourage students to take the internship option rather than to write a thesis. The thesis is still an option, but only 2 or 3 students have chosen this path over the past 4 years. In fact, the faculty now finds itself overseeing as many as 30 to 40 interns each year.

In the process of this change, faculty members have become more conscious of the value of internships, as well as the difficulties involved in ensuring high-quality clinical experiences for their students. They began to make efforts to get to internship sites for regular supervisory visits. They also became more sensitive about the need to clarify internship expectations and to share these clarifications with site supervisors, as well as with interns.

In 1989, the Leadership Program, through the doctoral director, was approached by the Danforth Foundation about the possibility of joining the Principals' Preparation Program. The timing was excellent, given the ferment of activities in the state and within the Leadership Program group. Planning began in the fall of 1989, and the program was initiated in May of 1990.

The College of Education has been highly supportive of the program since its inception. The dean and an associate dean serve on the program's advisory committee. Further, the dean, whose academic appointment is in the Educational Leadership Program, volunteered to be a field supervisor for eight of the initial group of students.

Description of the Program

The doctoral director, who is currently the department's chairperson, proposed a program that would emphasize a more intensive and purposeful selection process involving school districts as well as the university; experiential learning; cohort development; a planned internship component; and a broadening of perspectives through extensive exposure to the humanities. These key design elements became the foundation for the initiation and the continuing evolution of the program.

The planning and implementation for the program was assigned to a recently appointed faculty member. He developed a rough framework by the beginning of 1990 and made contacts with school-district leaders to seek their involvement in the selection of participants, placement of interns, and provision of release time for the internship experience.

The first cohort of 19 teachers was selected and began the 15-month program of studies in May of 1990. This group graduated at the end of the summer of 1991. A second group began its program in the fall of 1991 and will complete what has now been changed to a 24-month program at the end of the summer of 1993. A third cohort selected for admissions, also to a 24-month course of study, started during the fall of 1992. The intent is that there will be two overlapping cohorts from this time onward. The change to a 24-month program is the result of feedback from the first cohort. It was the group's perception that the program was excessively intense, particularly given other professional and family responsibilities.

From the outset, the faculty has sought the advice of school leaders. A group of district leaders was called together to respond to the program conceptualization. This informal relationship was formalized by the middle of the first cycle as the Danforth Advisory Committee. It is composed of key district-level and school-level administrators, Leadership Program faculty members, the dean and associate dean, community leaders (a cleric, a corporate training director, and a bank director presently serve on the committee), and, most recently, one graduate of the program from each participating district. The committee, which was formed to provide feedback for program planning, implementation, and modification, meets two or three times a year, with an average of about 15 members in attendance. To improve communications and networking, the committee includes the key contact person from each of the area's school districts.

Suggestions from the committee are used by the coordinator. For example, at the urging of the committee, a "community contact" day was created to provide opportunities for interns to network with leaders of community agencies, and an assessment is conducted about midway through the program.

This major partnering effort is supplemented by visits of the coordinator, approximately twice a year, to each of the participating school districts.

ACADEMIC CONTENT AND DELIVERY

There are six key aspects of the academic content and delivery. First, students take a 40-semester-hour master's program, which also qualifies them for certification if they pass the Florida Educational Leadership Examination, administered by the state's department of education. Because of this examination, the faculty has taken care to include the Florida basic leadership skills and competencies in course content and in the internship experience. The curriculum content is categorized into four areas:

- 3 foundations courses—measurement, research, and sociology
- 2 curriculum courses—theory and inquiry
- 7 courses in administration and supervision—organization and administration, systems planning and management, supervisory functions, supervisory techniques, law, instructional programs, and finance
- 1 course equivalent for the internship, which requires 30 field hours for each academic hour of credit; the internship require-

ment is now being increased from three to four academic credits
to represent more realistically the actual number of hours spent
in this activity

One or two Leadership Program courses are reserved exclusively
for students in the Danforth program each semester. This permits
focus on cohort development, as well as time to pass along necessary
information and to plan for events and activities. However, most
courses are shared with other students, to ensure that the cohort does
not become too isolated or view itself as an elite group. As might be
expected, tension does occur when other students observe the strong
esprit de corps demonstrated by the Danforth students.

The academic content and structure of the program is similar to
that found in other preparation programs. However, in an effort to
align the program with the enriched clinical experience, the faculty is
modifying the program on an evolutionary basis. For example, faculty members have agreed to include simulations, case studies, role
playing, reflective writing, and practitioner presentations on a regular
basis in their courses. They have also begun to assign field-based
projects such as shadowing administrators and writing up observations for seminar discussions, as well as requiring students to do a
variety of site-based diagnostic assignments on topics such as effective leadership and school climate. Finally, as a result of student
feedback, some aspects of the program are being changed. For example, the theory course is being moved to the doctoral level, and a new
course on educational trends is replacing it. Similarly, students are
being given group time in regular administration courses to synthesize learnings from foundations courses.

A second key aspect of the academic content and delivery is that
there is an expectation that Danforth students will participate in a
variety of other activities above and beyond the for-credit academic
courses, such as observations of school-board meetings and attendance at professional-development opportunities as they arise. For
example, the first two cohorts have participated in regional assessment centers for administrators to get diagnostic feedback about their
performance.

Most important, the program includes a strong emphasis on
humanities-related experiences. This element of the program is called

the "Renaissance strand." This strand, which is unique among the Danforth programs, was developed on the premise that educational leaders need to be able to view the role of the educational sector as but one element in the larger context of society. This requires exposure to and comfort with alternative ideas and cultures. The Renaissance strand expands students' understanding of the fine arts while introducing them to a variety of perspectives about education and society.

For example, during the current year, Renaissance strand activities included the Florida Symphony Masterworks Tchaikovsky Festival; the IV Annual Multicultural Seminar; the Third Annual Zora Neale Hurston Festival of the Arts and Humanities; an Orlando Magic NBA game; and an electronic music presentation. Interns also visited several of the county school systems; interacted with key leaders as diverse as directors in local school systems, school board members, professors, Danforth officials, and a guest from abroad who explored trends in British education; participated in roundtable discussions with principals to identify best practices; heard the views of former Governor of Massachusetts Michael Dukakis on educational reform; got Gerald Nadler's perspectives from his book, *Breakthrough Thinking*; and participated in a conference on initiatives for women in the fields of math and science. Faculty members from other units of the University of Central Florida have become involved with the program through presentations at Renaissance sessions.

With events averaging almost one per week, for which students presently receive no academic credit, the cohort is exposed to a variety of perspectives and approaches. The intent is to encourage them to question their own belief systems and to enrich their vision of what education is all about. They quickly begin to see parallels between the issues and organizational problems in their situations and those in other types of organizations. For example, after visiting a theatrical company's rehearsal of *Macbeth*, student insights included, "Comparing this play to contemporary professional ethics would make a great paper." "A scene . . . was repeated, adapted, and changed several times during rehearsal, which reminded me of how educators are involved in continuous evaluation of new ideas and themselves for lessons." "I could not help but think about how, like a principal, a director must have a vision."

In addition to group-based Renaissance activities, students are encouraged to identify other growth experiences for themselves. For example, one student attended services at a Catholic church and a synagogue because she had no prior knowledge of either religion. She felt that the experience expanded her understanding of both religious groups and made her more aware of the diversity of cultures that exist in her own community.

A third aspect of the program is multiculturalism, which is one of the objectives of the program, but there is no focus on it as a specific topic, other than in one of the foundations courses. Multiculturalism is explored in at least four ways, but in a naturalistic fashion: (a) Students in the program are fairly representative of the area's school racial/ethnic composition. In fact, the Leadership Program purposely seeks minority participation, encouraging school districts to recruit and select minority members. (b) Students, who come from diverse cultural settings, are encouraged to explore situations from their sites that relate to the curricular objectives of academic seminars. (c) The Renaissance strand purposely exposes students to a variety of cultures and points of view. (d) Internships are conducted outside of students' own schools. Students are required to have two different internship experiences, including one that serves students who are culturally different from those in the intern's home school.

A fourth aspect of the program is an emphasis on reflection and personal growth. In addition to opportunities for reflection and sharing in seminars and with mentors at internship sites, students are required to keep a record of their observations. The first cohort maintained a reflective journal, which the coordinator read, critiqued, and returned several times during the experience. Expanding on this activity, the faculty now requires students to develop a portfolio that is more highly structured and necessitates more systematic reflection. Guide sheets and forms are distributed to focus students' observations on specific phenomena and learnings. After students gather materials for their portfolios, small groups of students cooperate to synthesize learnings; videos are produced by these groups and shared with the rest of the cohort; the coordinator meets with the cohort to further synthesize learnings; and plans are in place for portfolio summaries to be presented to panels of educational leaders from the area. The current coordinator believes that the portfolios have helped students to focus and, as a result, to get more out of their preparation programs.

A fifth key design feature, cohort development, is highly valued by all parties. Students are unanimous in their support of this concept, especially as it relates to helping them succeed in a challenging program and as it relates to meeting highly talented individuals with whom they expect to interact long after the program is completed. In fact, as one graduate commented, the cohort has become a "sub-family, one that will be there for you when your own family can't understand what you are going through." Faculty members report that their courses profit by having students attend as cohorts. In particular, students are more proactive and challenge instructors to use interactive teaching methods to present important concepts and information.

A sixth and very strong element of the program design, evaluation, is conducted in a variety of forms. Student portfolios are reviewed, and alumni are asked for feedback in a 6-month check-up survey after graduation. Most important, from the outset, a professor from the instructional area of the College of Education has been working with the program as an evaluator. He observes seminars, reviews portfolios, and interviews students prior to, during, and after the program. Feedback from students and the faculty evaluator is shared with the program coordinators, who, in turn, use this information to make changes in the program. For example, as a result of feedback, the computer-technology course was moved from the end to the beginning of the sequence because Cycle 1 graduates felt that they needed to learn skills such as word processing to get through the program. The power of the cohort aspect was recognized and further emphasized. Additionally, the program was changed from 15 to 24 months to alleviate excessive participant stress. Finally, the number of hands-on, field-based exercises has increased, both within academic seminars and within the Renaissance strand.

Evaluation has become a program norm as a result of these positive outcomes. As such, the faculty is able to make modifications rapidly. Equally important, students in the program have come to recognize the importance of programmatic evaluation for effective educational leadership.

STUDENTS

The program is available to educators from the surrounding area, which includes Brevard, Lake, Orange, Osceola, Seminole, and Volusia county school districts. A selection process is pursued in each district. Principals are asked to make nominations. Even if candidates are self-identified, they must still get their administrator's formal support. Once nominated, interested teachers develop a file for review by a districtwide selection committee. If they pass through this screening process, they are invited to make an admissions application to the Educational Leadership master's degree program.

The 19 students in the first cycle came from four districts. Three districts identified individuals for the second cycle, but due to several last-minute dropouts, the 20 current members represent only two county systems. The Leadership Program has recognized the lack of broad-based participation and has been actively recruiting for the third cycle. As a result, it is anticipated that the cohort of 20 to 25 students in that cycle will come from five of the six surrounding school systems. Representation by participating school systems will be fairly proportional, with about 50% coming from the Orange County School District.

Aside from district selection and sponsorship, admissions procedures are fairly traditional, emphasizing academic potential. To qualify, a candidate must hold a Florida teaching credential, have taught a minimum of 2 years, possess a grade point average of 3.0 for the most recent 60 hours of academic work, provide a current résumé, a statement of career goals, and three letters of recommendation.

Those who make it through the selection and admissions process represent about one out of five of those who make inquiries. For example, in the first cycle, approximately 100 individuals in the Orange County system attended the Leadership Program's orientation session; about 35 made formal application, and 18 persisted through the nomination, selection, and admissions process.

Encompassing the first two cycles, participant demographics include 15% male to 85% female and about 72% European-American, 20% African-American, and 8% Hispanic-American. The male/female ratio is a concern to the faculty, but the majority/minority ratio is closer to the ethnic mix of the area and is much better than the general student population at the university (3% African-American and 2% Hispanic-American). The mix is also an improvement over the minority group the Leadership Program was able to recruit prior to the Danforth program.

There are no hard data regarding student quality. However, faculty members who teach courses that have one section for Danforth students and another for non-Danforth students feel that many of the Danforth students are better prepared, more focused, and more participative than other students.

For reasons beyond the Leadership Program faculty's control, there are only a few graduates placed in administrative positions thus far. Volusia County has placed its two candidates from the first cycle and expects to hire one or two more next fall, but this is an isolated situation.

Given extremely tight budgetary conditions, there has actually been a reduction in the region's administrative and teacher group. For example, as noted, due to budget constraints, the Orange County School District anticipates cutting as many as 600 employees during the coming year. Rather than finding positions for new administrators, the system may actually have to move current administrators back into classrooms. The district has even shut down its administrator pool system for this year, so graduates of the first Danforth cycle who came from this district have not been permitted to apply for administrative positions.

The long-term situation looks positive, given the population growth the region is experiencing. However, for the short term, it will be difficult for program graduates to find opportunities to move into administrative positions. It should be noted that districts are attempting to employ graduates in leadership positions, even though conditions are so negative. For example, some have been hired—particularly by their former mentors—for leadership roles, such as media specialists, that are not formally defined as administrative positions.

The Leadership Program maintains contact with alumni and is concerned about their continuing professional development, particularly given the negative hiring situation that currently exists. In this regard, a reunion was held last October, along with a meeting between the first and second cycle of participants. Some graduates are asked to serve on the Advisory Committee, and all alumni are invited to attend Renaissance strand activities.

INTERNSHIP

Students experience two internships, both of which occur outside their home school. Students in the first cycle received district-supported release time for 15 days of internship during the school year. During the summer, they interned at a second site, in either a year-round school setting or a district-level setting, for an additional 20 days. They received a payment of $50.00 per day for their summer internship efforts.

Due to budgetary reductions, this arrangement no longer is operational. The members of the second cycle are receiving, at best, 1 or 2 days of release time during the school year, and no pay for the summer experience.

In response to these worsening conditions, the Leadership Program has moved internship requirements to the summer months exclusively—12 days in each of the two summers that students are in the program. This modification will be reviewed to see how well it works. In addition, as part of the course requirements, the coordinator asks cohort members to shadow administrators for 2 days and to synthesize their observations as a course paper. Many students must take personal-leave days to be able to do this, but in return, they get field-based experiences that would not otherwise be available.

Specific elements of the internship aspect of the program include the following:

1. Students are recommended by their home school's principal, but they serve their internships in two other sites. The sites are at different levels, and at least one must be in a site that is at least 20% different in student demographics than those found at the intern's home school site.

2. The coordinator provides guidelines to interns and their supervisors for the internship experience. These encompass the Florida Department of Education's list of administrator

skills and competencies: leadership, decisiveness, mission and vision, information searching, concept formation, managing interactions, persuasiveness, delegation, motivation, personnel development, communication skills, and organizational sensitivity. Action plans are developed by the intern and the supervisor and approved by the coordinator.

3. Interns maintain portfolios that include a running record of internship experiences. These records are shared with the coordinator and are used to guide and modify intern activities, as appropriate.

4. Faculty members in the Leadership Program act as field supervisors. In part, this is because of scarce resources to hire adjunct faculty, and in part, it is due to the growing recognition of the importance of internship experiences. A recent policy approved by the faculty equates supervision of 9 to 12 interns to one course of teaching. This promotes high-quality supervision at an appropriate faculty/intern ratio, but it may also cause some difficulties in ensuring adequate course coverage as this effort becomes recognized as part of faculty members' work loads.

5. There are no regular reflective seminars, but there are other opportunities for review and analysis of field experiences. For example, opportunities are taken for reflection through reviews of portfolios; regular course time is used to discuss field experiences when cohorts constitute the entire student group; and there are get-togethers such as an occasional half hour prior to regularly scheduled classes, before or after Renaissance activities, and evening or Saturday morning sessions at the coordinator's home.

6. Supervisors, who are referred to as "mentors," are carefully selected. The process, which varies by district, generally consists of top-level central-office administrators making recommendations to the district's contact person with the university. That individual, who knows the principals well, may choose to reduce the list. Final selection is made by the program coordinator.

Serving as a mentor is viewed as an honor, but there has been no compensation for the effort thus far. The coordinator has now made arrangements for mentors to receive a tuition voucher for every 300 hours of supervision—good for up to four courses in a single semester.

The Leadership Program has offered training for mentors, but there has been little positive response to this offer. Besides being very busy, most mentors have had prior training in coaching skills and clinical supervision in their own school districts and feel that such training would be redundant. However, some do report that they would appreciate an orientation to the program and to the responsibilities and expectations of mentors.

Although they receive no extrinsic rewards for their supervisory activities, mentors report that they do receive significant intrinsic rewards, including the following:

- A chance to analyze and reflect on what they do so that they can explain it to their interns
- Having intelligent listeners to help clarify school-based problems
- Being kept up-to-date about what is happening in educational administration
- Having opportunities to network with professionals from other schools
- Having a potential impact on the coming generation of educational leadership

Mentoring is also viewed positively by students. Many report that interactions with their mentors are vital to them. In fact, many first-cycle graduates aggressively maintain links with their mentors. Some also note that they have developed strong mentoring relationships with their own principals, even though these principals are not permitted to be their formal mentors. Many of these home-site principals have taken the initiative to offer leadership-type experiences to faculty members who are in the cohort by, for example, encouraging them to participate on committees that are plan-

ning for and administering school effectiveness surveys, developing school-improvement projects, and planning dropout-prevention-
programs.

COORDINATION

Due to a series of situations, coordination of the program has
changed hands several times and will do so again when the next
cohort is admitted.

- The doctoral director developed the initial conceptualization
  for the program.
- A new faculty member was assigned responsibility for opera-
  tionalizing the program, but he left to take a position at another
  university several months after the first cohort was admitted.
- The doctoral director and an area principal who was hired to
  replace the first coordinator shared responsibilities for the re-
  mainder of the first cohort's program.
- The new faculty member coordinated the second cohort.
- A third cohort, which began its program in the fall of 1992, is
  coordinated by a faculty member who was an administrator in
  a midwestern state prior to joining the Leadership Program this
  academic year.

Given these rapid changes in leadership at a time marked by an
inability on the part of school districts to provide resources for internship activities and the unexpectedly poor job market for graduates, it
is impressive that the program has persisted, let alone retained its
basic intent and structure.

This continuity can be attributed to several factors. First, the
doctoral director, who is now the chairperson of the Educational
Services Department, maintained an active interest in and involvement with the program. Second, the Leadership Program's faculty has
been involved throughout and has provided support. For example,
one senior faculty member stepped into the breach to provide support
to students when the initial coordinator decided to leave. Third, the
individual selected to replace the first coordinator was a highly

respected principal from the area and knew the territory well. Fourth, the Advisory Committee closed ranks to provide necessary linkages with the districts while the faculty regrouped.

FINANCIAL ARRANGEMENTS

Program finances have been problematic. As noted, during the first cycle, local school systems did provide resources for release time and summer pay for interns. However, due to severe budgetary constraints, they have pulled back from this original commitment, jeopardizing the faculty's ability to ensure that students will have sufficient and appropriate time-on-task as administrative interns.

There is another resource issue. Danforth Foundation funds provided the Leadership Program with resources to initiate the Renaissance strand. However, these funds are no longer available, and substitute resources will have to be secured.

Students have been assisted with their tuition in a unique way. Teachers who supervise student teachers are provided with vouchers that can be used for one to four courses in a given semester. Recognizing this as a valuable resource, the coordinator encourages the university's teacher-education group to place student teachers with members of the cohort. These vouchers can also be obtained if cohort members are teachers in schools where faculties pool earned vouchers and make them available to faculty members wishing to pursue graduate studies.

Analysis

The program has been in operation for just 2 years. Still, much learning has taken place in this short time period. The Leadership Program is so pleased with results obtained thus far, even under less than ideal environmental conditions, that it is going to overlap cohorts, adding a new group each fall, to accommodate more students. There is some discussion about institutionalizing the Danforth model as the program's only approach to leadership preparation, which would certainly resolve the concern about elitism.

BENEFICIAL PAYOFFS

Payoffs for Students

The major payoff for students—being appointed to administrative—positions has been blocked because of budgetary constraints. However, even under the depressing conditions that presently exist, there has been some progress. Volusia County District has appointed both of its Cycle 1 graduates. In the Osceola County District, the two Cycle 1 members have successfully passed the principals' pool, and one or both will probably be appointed to administrative positions in the near future. The Orange County District has appointed Cycle 1 graduates to quasi-administrative positions, which places them in a good position to continue learning, gain exposure, and network, in anticipation of the day that the hiring situation changes.

There is recognition that the hiring dilemma is only temporary, given the rapid school-population growth in the area and the expected retirement of many senior administrators in the near future. For example, in the Orange County system, the press to fill leadership positions, particularly in elementary education and special education, is causing sufficient concern that the administrator pool may be selectively reopened.

Program participants value their experience. Those still in the program tend to be inward focused in what they appreciate (e.g., the power of the cohort and the diversity of the group, the intensity of the program and how that motivates them to stay with the task, the opportunity to shadow principals and assistant principals, and the expansion of perspectives gained through the Renaissance strand). Graduates, who are able to look at the experience from a distance, value the practical experiences they have gained; the dialogues with administrators from the region; the chance to meet key district personnel; the opportunity to be in a student cohort that is intelligent and lends support when needed; and the opportunity to work with professors who are academically challenging and who are positive role models. Some graduates also noted that they recognize personality changes—in other words, they feel that they have had a transformative experience!

Payoffs for Site Supervisors

Mentors enjoy having interns working with them, but they value them well beyond having a second pair of hands to perform tasks (e.g., elementary schools do not get an assistant principal until the student population passes 700). Because interns are not from their schools, mentors note that they gain a different perspective and get information about what is going on at other schools. They also have an opportunity to share concerns they probably would be hesitant to share if interns came from their own staffs. That is, there is a chance to process and reflect in confidence. Further, they recognize that mentoring is a professional growth opportunity, particularly as they reflect on their actions and explain them to the interns. In addition, several have noted that mentoring allows them to identify good people whom they might later recruit, as a few have already done, for positions in their schools. Finally, although many site supervisors do not feel sufficiently oriented to the role expectations of the university, they do appreciate the status and recognition that the university bestows on them by selecting them for this role.

Payoffs for School Districts

Partly because the program is so new, and partly because of the budgetary problems noted earlier, districts have been severely constrained from appointing graduates to administrative positions. Thus the bottom-line payoff that school districts surrounding other universities' Danforth programs have gained is not yet widely visible in central Florida school districts.

However, potential payoffs are recognized. A pool of talented educators is being identified and prepared for the leadership transition that will soon occur. The facts that there is a purposeful selection process and that the school districts are key participants in that process are viewed as important and positive changes by district leaders. Those school-district leaders who have participated in planning and delivery of the program recognize this and are well aware of the value to the districts. Their continuing participation and sponsorship is an indicator of this fact.

District leaders know that they must recruit talented ethnic and racial minority-group individuals for leadership positions, particularly given the rapidly changing demographics of the school population in central Florida. They appreciate the fact that the Educational Leadership Program is sensitive to this requirement and is doing a better job of recruiting and training such minority group members.

Payoffs for the University/College of Education/
Leadership Program

The university is a commuter institution with its student body coming from the local community. As such, relations with educational leaders in the area are particularly important. The Danforth program has fostered goodwill for the university, probably more than the university is aware of receiving.

The College of Education, as the primary unit that provides initial training and further development of educators in the region, appears to recognize the value of the program. The outgoing dean, who is a member of the Leadership Program, has been supportive from the outset, serving on advisory committees and supervising interns, as well as teaching students in his courses.

There has been some spill-over effect for other units in the College of Education. For example, the dean asked the current coordinator to make a brown-bag lunch presentation to the faculty regarding the cohort concept. The 20 faculty members who attended that meeting came away enthused about the ideas she shared. In fact, the undergraduate program in elementary education has shown an interest in adapting cohorts for their program. The coordinator also visited with the Instruction Services Department about the Danforth program's use of portfolios as an alternative approach to assessment. The Department has since asked for further information.

The Educational Leadership Program has benefited directly from the effort. The program's image with the educational community has been enhanced by the faculty's efforts to develop and maintain a program that holds the promise of positively affecting education in the region. Faculty members report increased and closer working relationships with district leaders who have participated in the program, particularly those who are on the Advisory Committee.

There have also been a number of spin-off effects that the faculty recognizes and appreciates. For example, faculty members are doing the following:

- Capitalizing on their experience with cohorts by developing cohort opportunities in the doctoral program
- Reviewing course sequencing, as well as content vacuums and duplications across courses
- Encouraging instructors to include hands-on field-based experiences as course assignments
- Planning course syllabi collegially when different instructors teach the same course at different times or on different campuses
- Considering leadership criteria as well as criteria related to academic ability when screening candidates for admissions

Overall, the program has led the faculty to get together more frequently to share concerns and to plan for program improvements. Retreats, which have become part of the culture, occur several times each year.

In short, what began as what one faculty member referred to as a "one shot deal" has become the norm. Planning and discussing the philosophy and the curriculum of the Leadership Program are now regular activities. Even the most senior faculty members have joined in the debate. One long-term veteran enthused, "The Danforth program is the first I've been involved with that looks like it is going to change things."

ONGOING ISSUES

As might be anticipated, implementation of the Danforth program has altered the status quo in ways that lead to the emergence of a number of issues that must be confronted. To one degree or another, the faculty is aware of these issues and is working to identify effective responses.

Academic Program

Much has been done to improve the academic program, including sequencing courses, adding field experiences as an integral part of academic expectations, and moving a course to the doctoral level to make room for another course that is viewed to be more appropriate for the master's level. Further, the Renaissance strand, which is unique to this program, represents breakthrough thinking about leadership development.

There are, however, still issues to be confronted. First, the curriculum content is still more typical of traditional administration programs than it is of the reflective practice experiences that are required to meet the changing definition of leadership in the schools. Some courses, such as law and finance, may not be required, at least not as full courses, for entry-level administration positions. Content and skill inputs for such topics as group dynamics, human resources management, and site-based management may need to be developed further.

Second, the curriculum includes an emphasis on multiculturalism, but it is more serendipitous than programmatic, emerging from discussions of students' field observations. There is little effort to focus on multiculturalism as a content area, other than whatever is included in foundations courses. Given the racial and ethnic mix in the region and in the cohorts, it may be important to consider such topic-specific content.

Third, traditional three-academic-hour curriculum blocks may need to be reexamined. It is probably not the most appropriate delivery system for innovative programs.

Changes can be anticipated. The faculty is exploring these issues and examining ways that learnings from the experience can be applied to the regular master's program as well as the doctoral program.

Recruitment and Admissions

Joint responsibility for student selection is a strength of the program. Ultimately, however, it is a process that is as weak or as strong as the ability and willingness of school-district leaders and principals to promote the program and encourage high-quality candidates to apply. The more the coordinator works closely with these individuals, the better the results are likely to be.

The admissions process could benefit from the development of criteria and data that provide evidence of leadership potential. As presently configured, the department's admissions process is fairly traditional, focusing on academic-success indicators. Interviews are conducted to establish candidates' motivation, but, beyond district nominations, there is nothing to indicate leadership potential. This is not an easy task, but it is an important factor that should be explored. For example, the assessment center that is presently part of the program might be modified and employed as a leadership criterion for admissions review.

Internships

Issues related to the internship experience must be resolved. First, the expectation of release time provided by districts no longer exists, eliminating the opportunity of internship activities during the school year for most students. This has created a situation in which there are few opportunities to bring academic seminars and field experiences together to compound learnings in both settings. Second, because the Leadership Program has had to restrict internship activities to the summer months, when interns are free of responsibilities, site-based dynamics that are cyclical and can only be gained during the academic year (e.g., opening and closing schools and participating in budget development) are not available to interns. Third, with the constraints of summer-only internships, now with no pay, the number of hours and days made available for this important activity are severely limited. The experience is down to 24 ten-hour days over two summers, for a total of 240 hours, which is far short of the 600-hour average of Danforth programs across the country. Learning the administrative role and gaining leadership perspectives require as much time-on-task as possible.

Several things might be helpful to ameliorate this problem. First, conducting orientation and follow-up sessions with mentors can help make them more aware of the need for hands-on experiences for interns. In some cases, they might be able to devise creative ways for more time-on-task for interns. At the very least, they should be sensitized to thinking about the means at their disposal to provide rich growth opportunities in any way possible. Second, the coordinator can formalize and expand on mentoring roles already being played by some principals from interns' home school sites. Third, some student contribution to the resources needed for release time may be necessary. Fourth, continuation of efforts to reestablish release time as a priority on the part of the districts might be worth exploring. Fifth, the Advisory Committee should be challenged to seek creative ways of overcoming the current lack of release days.

Finally, with loss of university-based funding to hire adjunct faculty members, field supervision has devolved onto the full-time faculty. A policy has been established to equate supervision of 9 to 12 interns to one course in each semester's load, but there is still an inequity among faculty. Some carry large supervisory loads, while others supervise only a few or no interns. This imbalance must be addressed, particularly given the agreement that all students will be encouraged to take an internship.

Placement

The Leadership Program has gained much goodwill and respect by initiating the Danforth program. However, if environmental conditions continue to frustrate graduates who want to move into administrative positions, there may be negative repercussions. Those interested in leadership roles cannot be expected to submit themselves to such an intensive program if there is little evidence of job-placement opportunities. As noted, some creative things are being done to identify administrative and quasi-administrative positions for program graduates. However, until environmental conditions change significantly, this issue will persist.

Unfortunately, as is true around the country, graduates of the Educational Leadership Program show little willingness to relocate to more promising areas. The Leadership Program may want to consider taking the initiative to educate graduates about opportunities that exist elsewhere. In addition, the faculty may find it useful to acquaint students with the variety of line- and staff-leadership roles beyond building management.

Financing

As the current recessionary climate passes, the Leadership Program will need to lobby to secure additional support from resource providers if it hopes to achieve its intended ends. Lack of funding for release days has already been noted as a problem. Further complicating matters, many students, to make ends meet, maintain part-time jobs in addition to their full-time positions. These resource problems make it difficult to secure the high-quality time needed to focus on the program. Although this problem is not unique to the University of Central Florida, it does seem to be particularly intractable there. As such, it places considerable constraints on achievement of program objectives.

The Renaissance strand has been supported in part by Danforth funds, which will no longer be available. Anticipating this, the coordinator is creatively identifying alternative resources and is securing inexpensive or free Renaissance events. For example, she has convinced the local opera company, which earns part of its income by giving concerts in schools, that it should offer its services gratis, using the persuasive argument that graduates will become principals and thus, potentially, paying customers. Similarly, she has asked the local bank representative on the Advisory Committee to identify donors among his many community connections.

Partnering

The faculty has made great strides in developing partnerships with the local educational community. Faculty members have asked for input regarding planning, implementation, and monitoring of the Danforth program via creation of the Advisory Committee, visits to district and school sites, and informal networking. It may now be time to expand partnering to other activities, including further refinement of the doctoral program. Partnering also enhances opportunities for the faculty to become more involved in the continuing professional development of administrators. The role of university-based programs is evolving beyond that of preparation. Given the Florida Department of Education's actions that make administrator induction and continuing development a district responsibility, the newly forged links developed by the Leadership Program could help it to stay centrally involved in the action.

Coordination

Leadership has shifted dramatically. The initial transition occurred because a faculty member left. The load recognition that the current coordinator receives, one course reduction for overseeing both the master's program and the Danforth program, is not sufficient. This explains the pending leadership transition. The coordinator, an untenured faculty member, needs to find time for research and for writing.

The result of such leadership shifts is that innovative programs may be jeopardized. Unless the faculty is able to maintain leadership for the program by providing sufficient load credits, as well as assistance in meeting or modifying institutional norms for research productivity, the program's future is uncertain.

Thus far, the faculty has coped well with the rapid transition of program leadership. In part, this is because the initiator of the program has remained involved, and in part, it is because the current coordinator, who was a local school administrator, is highly respected by school-district leaders. However, leadership of the incoming cohort group was turned over last summer to a new faculty member who recently arrived from the Midwest. He has participated in two regional Danforth meetings but has little knowledge about the geographical area or experience with the program.

Although there is something to be said for sharing the load, ensuring that faculty members are committed to and knowledgeable about the program, there comes a point of diminishing returns when leadership transitions occur too often.

In Closing

The Danforth program experiment at the University of Central Florida has provided the impetus for the faculty to work in a much closer partnership with educational leaders from the region. There have been difficulties, especially as related to resources, employment opportunities for program graduates, and rapid turnover in program leadership, but there is a widespread commitment among the faculty to persevere.

Out of the Jaws of Defeat

University of Connecticut

The Connecticut Alternative Program for Preparation of School Principals (CAPP) is one of the newest Danforth programs. In fact, the University of Connecticut joined the Cycle 4 Danforth programs in 1989 but did not field its first cohort until the summer of 1990. CAPP I, which included only four members, completed the program in the summer of 1991. CAPP II, which includes 15 members, is presently midway through the program, and CAPP III, which started in the fall of 1992, has 20 members. Thus from a slow start, momentum has steadily increased. The preparation program is being modified and strengthened in many ways, and area educators are increasingly attracted to participate in it. CAPP represents a unique case, in that program planners ran into many difficulties at the outset, difficulties that might have led others, planners with less commitment, to quit. However, the CAPP planners persevered, with the result that there is a major and positive difference in the way the university is going about preparing educational leaders. The present chapter explores CAPP's growth and development. After setting the scene, the program is described and critiqued.

The Setting

The university serves the entire state, which is the third smallest geographically in the nation, but with a population of about 3,300,000, which makes it the fourth most densely populated state in the country. The state's population is mainly concentrated in three medium-sized cities—Bridgeport, Hartford, and New Haven—and across the southwestern part of the state. Future population growth is expected to be heaviest in the eastern part of the state, but overall, the forecast is for relatively slow population growth over the next 2 decades.

It is anticipated that population increases will be proportionally concentrated among the elderly and that there will be an overall decline among school-age children. Within the school-age group, ethnic and racial minority representation is expected to grow, particularly among the Hispanic-American population. In 1960, there were 15,000 Hispanic-Americans in the state, but by 1990, that number had increased to 213,000. Currently, ethnic and racial minorities represent one in four of the state's more than 450,000 public-school students. The student population is slowly rebounding from a peak enrollment of 675,000 in 1971. Most students are concentrated in the state's largest cities.

Wealth is not evenly distributed: Connecticut has the highest per capita income in the nation but contains some of the poorest cities. Hartford is ranked as the 4th poorest city in the country, New Haven the 7th, and Bridgeport the 26th.

Unemployment, which is the lowest among the New England states, is still at about the national average and is most heavily concentrated among the urban poor. The way out of such a situation is at least partly dependent on the ability of the education sector to intervene by providing students with the basic skills required to participate more effectively in the state's highly technological economy. This economy is concentrated in the insurance industry, defense, and in the headquarters of many of the nation's leading corporations.

Connecticut, like other northeastern states, has been experiencing an economic downturn. The state's negative fiscal situation is causing problems for area school districts, as well as for the university, which is running into major resource issues as it tries to change its educational leadership preparation programs.

Befitting New England's tradition of keeping government close to the people, there are 169 school districts in Connecticut, all within approximately 2 hours of the university. These districts vary in size from a few hundred to about 25,000 in the three largest cities. Maintaining contact with so many school districts is a constant challenge to the university's School of Education.

The university was founded in 1881 as the Storrs Agricultural School. It became a land-grant college in 1893 and, after several name changes, became the University of Connecticut in 1939. About 120 major buildings and approximately 3,100 acres of land compose the main campus at Storrs. Academic centers are also located in Mansfield, Coventry, Willington, West Hartford, Farmington, and several other communities. There are more than 26,500 students, about 75% of whom are undergraduates and 25% of whom are graduate students. About 1,500 faculty are responsible for instruction, research, and service.

The School of Education houses a faculty of 80, divided among four departments—Curriculum and Instruction, Educational Leadership, Educational Psychology, and Health and Leisure Studies. The school serves 1,188 graduate students (M.A., sixth year, and Ph.D.), 268 undergraduates, and 89 teacher-certification program students.

The Department of Educational Leadership, which has been in existence since the mid-1980s, houses 21 faculty members, divided among four "Sections"—Adult Education, Higher Education, Educational Studies, and Educational Administration. Overall, the Department serves 48 M.A. students, 163 sixth-year (equivalent to Educational Specialist) students, and 202 Ph.D. students. The Educational Administration Section included eight faculty members when it was fully staffed, most of whom had been on site for 18 years or more. The one exception was the current CAPP director, hired in 1990. Due to several retirements, the group is currently down to six, including the department chairperson, who has a reduced teaching load, and the current Dean, who teaches one course for the section each year. The department has been authorized to search for only one new faculty member. This reduced group of faculty is responsible for the educational programs of 6 M.A., 145 sixth-year, and 105 Ph.D. students in the Educational Administration Section. Most of these students come from Connecticut, but a small number also come from adjacent states.

Readiness for Change

Discussions about program change first began in 1986. The dean and the associate dean, both of whom were faculty members from the Educational Administration Section, decided to return to the department in 1986. As they prepared for this transition, they discussed ways that leadership preparation for schools could become more responsive to the many national and state demands for reform of education. The associate dean explored the issue with one of his colleagues from a university that had just joined the Danforth program, and he concluded that associating with the program might help to stimulate change at the University of Connecticut. He spoke about this idea with the dean and with the department chairperson, both of whom agreed that the time was ripe to explore alternative approaches to leadership preparation. They agreed that the Danforth program might challenge the Educational Administration Section's faculty to consider changing their program design, content, and delivery. More than the money that would be awarded, they saw the value of joining the Danforth program as a way of engaging an established faculty in the creation of an alternative preparation model.

The existing program had remained unchanged, in part at least because there had been no new faculty appointments for almost 15 years. Realizing that there would soon be several faculty retirements, the planners wanted to think about program directions before getting on with faculty replacements, so that there would be a better fit when personnel changes came about. They also thought that the planning exercise required to become a Danforth program would provide a great opportunity to clarify and more distinctly separate the sixth-year and doctoral programs.

The by-then former dean contacted the Danforth Foundation, which sent an officer to campus in October of 1988. After an initial discussion, the foundation invited the university to join its fourth cycle of programs, and the university planning began in earnest in February of 1989.

The department's initiative fit well with the new dean's priorities, which included schools as professional development centers, urban experiences for the school's students, and, most important, expansion of the field component of preparation programs. He also was in agreement with the planners' belief that dollars were not the objective. Rather, he saw joining the Danforth program as a way of stimulating faculty members to reprioritize purposes and programs.

A senior faculty member who was asked to be the program coordinator decided to start from an established partnership base with a group of school districts, referred to as "UGEMS" (University, Glastonbury, Enfield, Manchester, and South Windsor), that he and others had worked with closely on other projects. Two administrators from these districts accompanied him to a Danforth meeting in Oklahoma, which helped them learn more about the intent of the program and which strengthened the partnership between the university and the involved districts.

The coordinator established a committee composed of the four districts' superintendents to discuss and agree on key program design elements. Maintaining the dialogue was difficult. The time required for this activity proved to be too much for the superintendents, who felt pressured by the many other priorities demanding their attention.

However, some important agreements were forged. For example, based on prior agreements by member districts, an agreement was made to expose future leaders to mentors and sites in districts other than their own. Further, based on the trust and working relationships that had already been established, the superintendents agreed to participate in a school-district/university partnership to initiate the new program. After the discussions of the first year, the partnership grew to seven districts and is now statewide.

The slow initiation of the program was due in part to a downturn in the state's economy and its impact on districts' willingness to provide funds for release time. In part, it was also due to the attractive salary level and working conditions of Connecticut school-district leaders, which results in a highly competitive situation wherein there are many applicants for every administrative opening. Given this reality, it is not surprising that school boards hesitated to provide funds for leadership development. In fact, it has taken an effort on the part of the faculty to get superintendents' commitments to be partners in the development of leaders and to convince their lay boards to become involved.

The initial CAPP design called for an intensive program contained in four semesters (summer, fall, spring, and summer), and a 90-day internship, to be taken full-time during the spring semester. The funds that would be required to cover substitutes for interns' release days proved to be too costly for most districts, many of which were facing severe financial difficulties due to state budget reductions. Both the magnitude of this problem and the late planning start led to the decision to delay the program for 1 year.

As planning continued during the 1989-1990 academic year, the partnership was expanded to include eight districts. Seven agreed to support two candidates each, but as it became clear that there would be a second year of bad budget news, four decided to delay their involvement. Of the remaining four districts, one had no applicants, another did not feel that it had highly qualified candidates, and two agreed to pay only half of the 90-day internship release for two candidates. The candidates were required to pay the other half out of their salaries (prorated over the contract year). The outcome was an initial cohort of four students, who began their program in the summer of 1990.

A Danforth Foundation official met with the state's education commissioner to establish an understanding that, although the program had not yet been approved, candidates would still be eligible for state certification. Subsequently, a letter was issued by the state's department of education, ensuring waivers for CAPP graduates.

With approval from the state's department of education and a few districts ready to participate, the faculty decided to go ahead with the program, even though the cohort was quite small, and the quality of candidates was mixed. The faculty decided to initiate the program, with the knowledge that the design would have to be modified during the start-up year to increase the quality and the size of the second cohort. These changes, which have had the hoped-for effect, included a program of six semesters over 2 years rather than four semesters over 15 months; internships of 90 days, but spread over 2 years and including summer months, rather than being restricted to one semester; minimal costs to school districts; and a willingness to negotiate regarding when intern release days occur.

The current coordinator joined the faculty a month after CAPP I began and became co-coordinator for that cohort. When CAPP II began, she became the sole coordinator.

Planning for needed modifications, which began soon after her arrival, involved practitioners as well as the program co-coordinators. The deadlock over the 90-day block of internship time was broken when the problem was rephrased as one of ensuring high-quality clinical experiences, rather than of maintaining a solid 90-day clinical block of time. This opened up thinking to include a variety of clinical-experience configurations. Finally, the new coordinator suggested what one of the practitioners refers to as a "chunked up" model that was readily agreed upon. There is still an expectation of 90 internship days, but they are divided over 6 semesters, with a minimum of 15 days in each of 2 academic years and a maximum of 30 days in each of two summers.

Description of the Program

The program design pursued during CAPP I required four intensive semesters, one of which was devoted to a full-time internship. However, because budget constraints severely limited the possibility of maintaining such a program, the design was modified. It is likely that it will be further modified on the basis of experience and changing conditions.

The current design was planned by the coordinator with input from leading practitioners and some faculty members. The coordinator's intent was to create a program based on the assumption that schools are changing and will continue to change. Administrators who lead such organizations will require preparation programs that are more responsive to changing realities than is true of traditional preparation programs. The academic and field components of the program described here are based on these beliefs. Students take a 31-semester-hour course of studies, which qualifies them for a sixth-year diploma. It also qualifies them for state certification. The state's department of education requires 15 semester hours for state certification, 9 of which must be in educational administration, but the Educational Leadership Section requires its students to take 21 semester hours, 15 of which must be in educational administration. Further, the section will not recommend students for state certification unless they complete the entire 31-hour program of studies.

State certification requires 5 years of teaching, but at present, it does not require an internship. Certification changes, which are likely in about 2 years, will include an internship requirement and will also establish candidates' knowledge based on a set of administrative competencies, rather than on completion of an approved program. This proposed modification may challenge the university to come up with a creative response.

At present, the 31-hour, 2-year program is organized as follows:

Credits

Fall I:
    Administration of Educational Organizations   3
    Practicum (Internship)   1

Spring I:
    Program Development   3
    Practicum (Internship)   1

Summer I:
    Supervision/Evaluation/Staff Development   3
    Internship   3

Fall II:
    Principalship I (Modules)   3
    Practicum (Internship)   1

Spring II:
    Principalship II (Modules)   3
    Practicum (Internship)   1

Summer II:
    Internship   3

Other requirements that can be taken as time permits (even after the 2-year time limit):

Educational Psychology course on learning   3
Educational Law   3
Total =   31

This sequenced set of academic experiences is significantly different from the traditional program, which could be taken according to students' time availability and which required only five specific courses, with the rest being electives. This typical smorgasbord approach minimized opportunities for peer-group development and left the responsibility for synthesis and sense-making entirely up to the students.

CAPP is an attempt to overcome these deficiencies. Although the list of academic experiences looks similar to those found at most universities, there are nine major differences: First, some of the courses are team taught, bringing a leading practitioner together with a university faculty member. The intent is to blend theory and concepts with experience and practice. About 25% of the academic content is delivered by field leaders, who are awarded adjunct instructor status by the Educational Leadership Department.

A second major distinction is that academic offerings are limited to CAPP participants, except during the first summer, when other graduate students take the supervision course with CAPP students.

Third, there is an important difference in the way the first year and the second year of the academic program are offered. During the first year, content is enriched by heavy emphasis on case studies and role playing, but it is delivered in the traditional course format (i.e., there may be guest presenters, but for the most part, content is organized and delivered by the professor of record). However, during the second year, while content is organized by courses for the convenience of dealing with the university's registration system, content is really presented in modules and is delivered by a variety of university and field leaders. These modules target instruction to students' learning needs, with content delivered for as long as is required, rather than according to the university's course-structuring system demands. For example, personnel evaluation may require three sessions of several hours each, while site-based budgeting may require six such sessions. Close attention on the part of the coordinator is necessary to make the module approach work well.

A fourth major distinction is that most of the academic content is delivered in school settings. The campus is in a relatively rural setting and is a long distance away from most students. Even more important, the faculty recognizes the value of meeting in schools because they are the organizational settings being examined. In addition, by meeting in school sites, school leaders can more easily participate in academic sessions. Further, because many of these sites have become proficient in their use of computers for gathering, storing, and retrieving information, students often have access to facilities such as computer laboratories at these sites.

Fifth, field trips are organized at the request of students. For example, visits are made to special programs, community agencies, and legislative hearings.

Sixth, above and beyond assignments in individual courses, long-term projects are assigned by the coordinator during both years of the program. These projects provide opportunities for students to experience the planning and leadership roles of administrators. Normally, internship activities enable students to become acquainted with the daily management functions that administrators perform but do not provide much opportunity to become sensitive to the longer-term leadership functions that effective administrators pursue.

To compensate, students are required to conduct a school/community study during the first year, and a leadership project during the second year. During the first year, students are given a set of questions about the community and are required to work with their mentors to get answers, synthesize information, and submit a report.

The community study provides the background needed to conduct a leadership project at the school site during the second year. The leadership project can be about almost anything, but it must fit the needs of the school site. For example, one intern is developing an integrated resource-based approach to teaching in the school library. Another is creating a design for professional development for her site's faculty members.

A seventh major distinction is that students are encouraged in several ways to reflect on their internship experiences:

1. Journals are maintained throughout the experience, and students are required to summarize "critical incidents" that occur during their internship activities, as well as to record thoughts, feelings, and other learnings that they experience.

2. Students keep a "log," which is basically a format for recording how they spend their time at the internship site. These logs are shared with mentors, field supervisors, the coordinator, and sometimes with district superintendents.

3. Students develop portfolios, which include autobiographical summaries, professional-development plans, statements of professional philosophy or educational platforms, transcripts, letters of recommendation, lists of professional memberships, résumés, awards, papers, and even videos of research done on educational programs at internship sites. The portfolio is intended to show growth and to establish a resource file for use when interns interview for jobs. Portfolios are shared among the cohort, revised, and presented to a group of mentors and faculty at the end of the second year. They are also reviewed by the coordinator when assigning a final internship grade.

4. Monthly reflective seminars are held, beginning in the spring of year 1 and running through the end of the program (CAPP I, which contained all internship experiences in one semester, held reflective seminars biweekly for that semester). Student attendance is not, at present, required. Mentors are invited and encouraged to attend these sessions. Interns are urged to share critical incidents that they recorded in their journals, and peers and mentors are invited to offer their diagnoses and their suggested responses to these situations.

An eighth major distinction is that cohort development is pursued in different ways. For one thing, students take all courses together, mostly in situations where they are the only members. Reflective seminars bring the cohort together for sharing about internship experiences, while social activities are held occasionally to further enhance personal and professional networking. The coordinator is also planning a retreat early in the fall, to promote team building.

The ninth of the nine major distinctions is that evaluation is an ongoing concern, which is particularly appropriate, given the sense of urgency about modifying and improving the program design. The coordinator regularly converses, by phone and in person, with faculty, students, mentors, and other district sponsors, seeking their input about the program and its effectiveness. Further, she requires students to spend the last 15 minutes of class time writing in their journals, responding to questions she poses about content and its delivery and what might need to be modified or added. She also asks them to share their thoughts verbally regarding the class experience.

In fact, the program is changing as it is being presented. There is an openness and a positive attitude about program change. Given the newness of the program and the need to experiment at this early stage, this openness is especially healthy and important.

STUDENTS

Originally, the CAPP cohort was limited to the four UGEMS school districts. The first-year students came from two of these districts. The number of eligible districts increased to eight in the second year, and students came from seven of these. The faculty now advertises the availability of the program statewide and will accept students from all of the state's 169 school systems.

Students are nominated by their home districts, but this nomination process varies widely in structure and in intensity. Some districts seek out highly qualified candidates, require development of a comprehensive application file, and set up districtwide screening committees to sort out and prioritize candidates. Others are just beginning to recognize the importance of this responsibility. One urban center, which in 1991-1992 merely passed along the names of all interested staff members to the university, has now accepted responsibility for conducting initial screening.

As the program has been restructured and more educators have heard about it, the number of applicants has increased rapidly. CAPP I had only four applicants from two districts, all of whom were admitted. CAPP II had 37 applicants from seven districts, 15 of whom were selected. CAPP III applicants numbered more than 50 from 42 districts. Thus there was a 100% acceptance rate for CAPP I, but the acceptance rate for CAPP II was reduced to 41%, and CAPP III was of a similar rate. Excitement is growing as word spreads about the university's challenging program and its appropriateness for the leadership needs of the state's school districts. Interestingly, some CAPP III applicants have noted that they were encouraged to consider the program by CAPP II cohort members.

The identification of eligible candidates, now that the program is available statewide, is highly dependent on the support of educational leaders. The coordinator sends a letter to all district superintendents and to a targeted group of principals who have established reputations as exceptional leaders, asking them to nominate candidates. Once nominated, interested applicants must obtain recommendations from their principals and superintendents. The coordinator then checks with nominating districts to be sure that resources will be made available for release time if candidates are selected.

After the district screening and nomination process is completed, candidates submit a regular admissions application to the department. They also submit writing samples, as well as recommendations from peer teachers, their building principal, and a district administrator. They are then interviewed by a selection committee composed of field leaders (typically a principal and a superintendent) and department faculty. The selection committee probes for motivation, focus of intent, and leadership potential. As a final step, the list is informally submitted to the faculty for approval.

Cohort demographics for CAPP I and II include 32% male and 68% female; and 79% majority/21% minority (2 African-Americans and 2 Hispanic-Americans).

At present, one of the four CAPP I graduates has become an assistant principal; one is a finalist for several administrative positions; another has become a middle-school department chairperson; and the fourth has been unable to get any finalist interviews.

It is difficult to establish the extent to which CAPP students will obtain administrative positions once they graduate. Two factors are involved in the problem. First, the overall environment for job placement is mixed. Over the past 2 years, the trend has been toward a large turnover of principals. This trend is likely to continue for some time, but it will be adversely affected by several other realities. Connecticut's compensation package for public-school administrators is high, compared to many other states, so many highly qualified applicants compete for positions as they open up. In addition, due to budget difficulties, many districts are cutting back on administrative positions, particularly assistant principals, which is the entry-level role that is most available to those graduating from CAPP. As these entry-level positions are eliminated, those presently in them become strong competitors because CAPP graduates have little or no comparable experiences to offer potential employing school districts. Second, the quality of CAPP I students was quite mixed. The placement record reflects this mixed quality.

The nomination and selection process for CAPP II appears to have resulted in an overall improvement in cohort member quality. As an indicator, even though CAPP II is only midway through the program and formal job searches have not yet begun, three of the cohort's members have already been approached by their districts to take on full-time administrative roles next fall.

After graduation, the coordinator maintains informal contact with CAPP members, calling to see how they are doing and how she might be of help. In addition, she plans to hold a *charla*, which is Spanish for "lively conversation." The charla, which will be open to graduates, mentors, and current students, is intended to encourage continued contact and to promote learning. A hot topic will be identified, reading materials will be distributed, and participants will be brought together to explore issues related to the topic.

INTERNSHIPS

Finding resources to provide sufficient time-on-task in clinical settings has been a major problem. The initial intent of 90 continuous internship days during the academic year, all of which was to be sponsored by school districts, almost led to the demise of the program. The attempt to maintain this intent led to a CAPP I cohort of only four members, and even this small group of students had to pay half of the release time from their own salaries.

The response to this early experience has been both creative and problematic: *creative*, in the sense that it increased the likelihood of the program's continuation and opened the possibility of redefining ways that quality clinical experiences might be gained, and *problematic*, in the sense that it has led to a wide disparity in the quality and time-on-task for interns. As one mentor noted, "Nothing teaches like being there. You can't feel it unless you are there. Administrators need to know this part."

The eight specific elements of the internship experience include the following:

First, students serve with one mentor over the entire experience, unless special arrangements are made for additional experiences with secondary mentors. Mentor/intern pairings are established by the coordinator, but students have a say about the kinds of internships they want.

Second, interns' clinical experiences take place in districts other than their own. This arrangement is based on a historical precedent—the cooperative internship arrangements established by UGEMS. Cross-district internships are not a major problem for participating districts because they have long raided each others' staffs for leadership positions. Agreeing to this arrangement was viewed as nothing more than formalizing a common practice. In fact, this cross-district experience is well-liked by all participants. Students are able to observe and participate in educational settings different from their home districts, and receiving districts are able to gain by the outside perspectives that interns bring and share.

Third, internships still total 90 or more days. Because of lack of resources available for release time, only a minimum of 30 of these days occurs during the regular academic year (15 in the first year—1 or 2 just prior to Christmas break in the fall semester, and the rest in the spring semester, and 15 more days are spread over the second year of the program). How these 30 days are organized varies widely. Some interns make arrangements for single days about once a month. Others are able to arrange to be on site for 2 to 5 days at a time. Some students also use sick leave and vacation time to increase the number of days available for internship activities during the school year.

Even with such enhancements, the number of days is not sufficient. If interns spread their time across the year, they get a feel for the flow of school-based events, but they lose the opportunity to become deeply involved, to see situations evolve and to finish complex activities. If they choose to concentrate their internship time, they are able to participate in the flow of the school's life but lose the overall seasonal evolution of school dynamics. Both choices are recognized as problems by mentors and interns. The remaining 60 days (which can be reduced if additional days are found for clinical experiences during the regular academic year) are taken for 30 days during each of the program's two summers. Interns are required to work with their mentors during the 5 days after school dismisses and the 5 days before school reopens. The other 20 days are negotiated between the intern and the mentor. In some cases, problems arise when mentors, most often elementary principals, are not under district contract for the summer months. During CAPP II, as many as 5 of the 15 mentors were not on duty, and the coordinator had to scramble to identify alternative internship situations.

Summer internship activities typically include planning and scheduling for the next academic year and corresponding with faculty and community. In addition, some mentors take interns to administrator meetings and to professional-development activities. Others seek out alternative experiences for interns, such as participating in or directing summer program activities that the district is pursuing. In short, there are a variety of approaches for the use of summer internship days.

Fourth, the coordinator provides a handbook for interns and mentors to use in establishing interns' clinical activities. The handbook describes the program and its academic content and explores the roles of interns, mentors, and university supervisors. It also provides guidance for assessment and reporting the results of the experience.

Interns, working closely with their mentors, have been charged with the responsibility for establishing objectives and priorities for the experience. The coordinator and faculty, who serve as supervisors, encourage interns to focus on skill and knowledge areas they are most in need of developing. However, because they have little basis on which to make these decisions, there is wide variance in how this responsibility is fulfilled. After the intern and mentor agree on a set of objectives, the objectives are reviewed by the university supervisor, who may suggest modifications that seem appropriate.

Fifth, as noted, interns maintain logs and journals, which provide written records of internship activities. Their portfolios also contain written products from the internship experience. These three writing artifacts help to provide a holistic perspective of the exercise.

Sixth, field supervision, which is conducted by Educational Leadership faculty, occurs about four times per year, when interns are on site. Supervisors meet in triads with mentors and interns to help clarify purposes and assess progress. They also provide feedback for the coordinator, apprising her of problematic situations that require attention before they get out of hand. However, due to a variety of factors, the system does not always work effectively. These factors include supervisors' lack of preparation for the role, and in some cases, their lack of experience as an administrator (or at least of current administrative experience), and competition for their time by other high-priority responsibilities such as teaching and research. The coordinator is reviewing the situation and will probably shift supervisory duties away from the faculty in favor of one or more educational leaders from the schools. Regardless of who conducts the activity, the coordinator will also have to provide training and clarify expectations for the field supervisor's role.

Seventh, reflective seminars, held once a month, provide opportunities for interns and mentors to explore situations that have occurred in the schools. Interns value these sessions highly, but they feel that such sessions should occur with greater frequency, in part at least because they would like to discuss site dynamics closer to the time when they actually occur. There is also some concern that mentors tend to monopolize the reflective seminar conversations, partly because they have so much to share, and partly because interns may be more comfortable listening than taking the risk to share their own insights.

Eighth, mentors are nominated by central office administrators (superintendents, personnel directors, and sometimes others, such as special education directors). The coordinator reviews nominations and résumés and asks department faculty members and key educational leaders to share their views about the nominees. After eliminating questionable candidates, she asks remaining nominees for a packet of information about their districts and their schools. She then visits each candidate to get a sense of the educational setting and to conduct an interview with the individual.

Those who survive this screening process are placed in a mentor pool and may be called on if interns' career interests fit the setting and if the coordinator senses that a good pairing can be made.

There are no extrinsic rewards for being a mentor, but the department does encourage mentors to attend any learning situations that are created for interns, including guest speakers, dinners, reflective seminars, and the planned-for charla session. Mentors also receive some of the texts that students use, as well as copies of handouts from classes. This encourages mentors' professional growth and enables them to stay in close touch with the knowledge and skills their interns are receiving at the university.

CAPP I mentors were offered the opportunity to participate in a 3-day mentor-training workshop conducted by the Connecticut Principals' Academy, which is sponsored by the state's department of education, for master principals who volunteer to mentor new principals. The workshop costs the program about $550 for each mentor who attends. Two of the four chose to do so, and both felt that the experience was valuable. However, such costs are prohibitive for training larger numbers of mentors, so the coordinator arranged for CAPP II's 15 mentors to be given a half-day orientation session in October, during which time they received a copy of the intern and mentor handbook and heard a panel of CAPP I mentors describe their experiences and offer suggestions. At midpoint in the program, mentors are brought together again to explore how the internship experience is going and to offer suggestions for program improvements.

As might be expected, the mentoring experience for CAPP I, which called for a solid 90 days on site, and CAPP II, which may have interns on site for as little as 15 days spread over the year, are quite different. One mentor who worked with both CAPP I and II interns felt that the time on site for the first intern allowed him to involve the intern in meaningful activities, whereas the sporadic fieldwork the second intern is able to garner does not promote a high level of comfort and trust between mentor and intern.

Mentors vary in their interest and willingness to work with interns. Variations have to do with their time availability (some have assistants to conduct activities while they focus on interns' needs, but others do not), as well as with the intern's ability to be on site when important activities are undertaken. However, the way they go about mentoring also appears to be related to the extent to which they fully understand the mentor's role. For example, some appear to be more sensitive to the coaching function than are others; some share their reflections more readily than do others; and some seek good learning opportunities for their interns more frequently than do others. It appears that more efforts are necessary to prepare mentors for their roles. There is also the need to clarify the field supervisors' role and, in the long run, to clarify how all of the roles—intern, mentor, field supervisor, and coordinator—are intended to be conducted.

COORDINATION

There have been two CAPP coordinators. The first, a senior faculty member, took on the role mainly because he was asked to do so. He coordinated the program through the difficult early phase— initial program design and partnership development with school districts.

The second coordinator, a newly appointed faculty member, joined the department with the understanding that she would take on this role. Her previous experience as a principal and her own enthusiasm about and commitment to the development of a field-based preparation program were important attributes. In addition, she brought new ideas to the program discussion. For example, she encouraged greater involvement of city districts and suggested an effective way around the 90-day internship issue. Her energy and facilitative style have led faculty members and educational leaders in school districts to join her in the growth and evolution of the program.

The fact that she served as a co-coordinator for the first year, with the senior faculty member who was initially responsible for the program, was also an important factor. This cooperative arrangement permitted her to get to know key educational leaders in the state and to establish a positive relationship with them for the future.

The university formally provides 50% of the coordinator's time for her CAPP role. However, the additional teaching and adminis-trative duties she performs result in a university contribution that is really much lower than that level. In fact, at the dean's request, the coordinator also oversees other activities—until now at six profes-sional development schools, and starting next year, in a new bilingual project. She also teaches two courses in the Educational Leadership Section each academic semester, and she advises sixth-year and doc-toral students. Further, no staff support was provided for CAPP until the summer of 1992, when 10 hours per week of graduate assistant time were reserved for this activity.

In short, thus far, a good extent of the coordination activity has been done on overload. This is an important transition time for the program, going from the planning stage to a very small program the first year, and moving now toward a more comprehensive program-matic stage. As the program moves from idea to innovation, and then to institutionalization, resources will have to be provided to maintain the program.

For the future, the Educational Leadership Department Chairper-son and the Educational Administration faculty recognize the need to maintain high involvement of faculty in the program, as well as the need for the current coordinator to have time to focus on her own research and teaching as she comes closer to a tenure decision. In this regard, the chairperson plans to involve a senior faculty member in the program for CAPP III and to hire a new faculty member as soon as possible, who also has experience and interest in the principalship and who may be able to serve as a CAPP coordinator.

FINANCIAL ARRANGEMENTS

Program finances remain a major problem. During the first year, districts and interns shared the cost of 90 days of release time to cover the funding of substitutes for internship experiences. Release time is now paid by school districts but has been reduced to 15 days for each of 2 years. This arrangement jeopardizes the program's objective of sufficient high-quality time-on-task for interns. Until the state's econ-omy improves and additional state budget funds are made available, this problematic situation will continue.

Tuition at the university is relatively high, costing about $8,000 for the 31 hours the program requires. Students pay for tuition, but based on established norms for professional development of Connecticut school personnel, most districts refund about 50% of tuition costs. However, because some districts in the state do not have such a refund policy, the high tuition cost may be a major barrier for some who would otherwise apply to the program.

The university's contribution is in the form of load time for the coordinator.

The Danforth Foundation has contributed to the program by providing finances over the first several years to take care of start-up and support costs such as special enrichment activities and social gatherings. These funds will soon be depleted, and other sources will have to be found to support this important function.

Analysis

The University of Connecticut is still finding its way toward effective program change, graduating one small cohort and then reshaping the program for the present cohort. Based on the belief that it is the right thing to do and the confidence on the part of the faculty in the improvements already demonstrated, two important decisions have been made. First, the traditional program is being closed to new admissions. Students from other departments will be permitted to take courses to fulfill certification requirements, but admissions to a sixth-year program in educational administration will only be through the CAPP program. Second, to fulfill student credit-hour expectations now that the traditional program has been dropped, cohorts will overlap. An additional cohort started in the fall of 1992, as the current cohort moved into its second year of the program.

The faculty's decision to institutionalize CAPP also aligns the university with future certification requirements. The state's department of education will be changing its certification regulations in a few years to include a planned internship.

In addition, the fact that prospective students who do not wish to take the CAPP program can turn to other universities in the area also makes it more feasible to institutionalize the program. These other institutions include the University of Hartford, Fairfield University, the University of Bridgeport, and Sacred Heart University, which are private, and Central Connecticut State University, Southern Connecticut University, and Rhode Island College, which are public.

The faculty's responsiveness to suggestions for change and improvement has been positive. They are aware that there is still some way to go before all of the pieces come together in a tight fit, but many benefits have already accrued.

BENEFICIAL PAYOFFS

Payoffs for Students

The program is still in its infancy, so payoffs that students recognize are short range, rather than long term and career placement focused. It is too early to document whether the major payoff, finding an administrative position, will come about for most graduates. However, it is clear that this is a major motivator for cohort members. The next 2 years, during which time CAPP II members will graduate and CAPP III members will begin exploring the job market, will be an important time for the continued health of the program. The coordinator will need to maintain accurate records of placement so she can monitor the situation.

Although most CAPP members are concerned about the juggling act that is required to fulfill all of their roles (e.g., being teachers, spouses, parents, students, and interns) while taking this intensive program, they recognize the positive elements of the experience. Most frequently mentioned are

- The practical, hands-on experience (as one student noted, "Not just more course work!") they are getting with excellent mentors at their internship sites—learning opportunities that are enhanced because field sites are outside their own districts
- The adult learning approach taken in most of their classes
- The use of case studies, role playing, team projects, and site-based activities as assignments
- Courses in which professors team up with practitioners (causing, as one member stated, "positive cognitive dissonance")
- The sensitivity of professors to students' difficult challenges, as well as professors' willingness to listen and modify activities when appropriate
- The support of cohort members and learning from them, both of which are quite helpful in getting through the program
- The opportunity to "stand on the other side" and see teachers from the administrator's perspective

- Reflective seminars in which principals join with them to share insights

Payoffs for Site Supervisors

Mentors are positive about their participation. Many speak of the wonderful opportunity to become more reflective about their leadership styles and decision-making behaviors. As one noted, it is an exercise in "metacognition—it makes me aware of what I do as I translate it to others." Similarly, they appreciate the chance to test their ideas against interested and bright novices before putting the ideas into action. Some speak of the joy of being a teacher and sharing things they know and do well to help others grow and, in the long run, to be of help to those interns who will touch in their own careers. In addition, there is recognition of the opportunity to brush up on current thinking about educational administration as they follow interns' programs and listen to them talk about ideas being discussed in their home districts.

Even those who have had weaker interns tend to recognize the positive outcomes that can be gained. Although one mentor noted that having a poor candidate "leaves me frustrated, a baby sitter," another noted, "I grew as a result of his deficiencies. They required me to sharpen my skills to give corrective feedback. His presence also got teachers to appreciate more what administrators in this building do for them."

Payoffs for School Districts

Because only one CAPP graduate is presently in an administrative position, it is difficult to gauge the eventual impact of these alternatively trained individuals. However, even given this reality, district leaders are aware of the potential for long-term positive outcomes. It is clear to these leaders that a different kind of preparation is required for leaders who will move their districts' schools into the next generation, and they believe that CAPP is on the right track in its approach. They are also aware of more direct and short-term positive outcomes, including professional growth opportunities for their midterm professional staffs (Connecticut educators, on average, have been in place for almost 15 years); the opportunity for site-based administrators to share their knowledge and skills by becoming mentors; and the fact that site-based management and restructuring leads to the need to prepare teachers to play leadership roles in schools, even if they stay in the classroom.

An interesting spill-over benefit has also occurred for the UGEMS districts. After coming together to work in a trusting environment to get CAPP started, the districts built on the experience by cooperating on a shared cable-network project. This project has teachers making presentations across districts for classroom enhancement, provides professional-development opportunities that would probably be too expensive for most of the state's hard-pressed districts to afford, and brings a junior college and a local hospital into interagency developmental activities with participating districts.

Payoffs for the University/School of Education/ Educational Leadership Department

The current president of the university has his faculty home in the Educational Leadership Department, so he is fully aware of the value of CAPP. In fact, he has sponsored social events for CAPP and, more important, has authorized the department to fill a replacement position, even though other units in the university are not being permitted to do so under the budgetary constraints that currently exist.

For the School of Education, CAPP fits well with current emphases such as urban education experiences for students and extended field-based experiences as integral elements in graduate preparation programs. The dean recognizes that CAPP is an excellent prototype for other programs that he is encouraging departments to create.

The Educational Leadership Department, and in particular the Educational Administration Section within the department, is beginning to reap benefits from the major effort and risks it has taken to get the program off the ground. Applications to CAPP have increased dramatically, a new faculty member is in place who is recognized by practitioners as committed to principal preparation and who is enhancing the image of the department in the field, and sixth-year program revisions are improving the department's ability to meet the changing leadership requirements that exist in school districts.

There have also been some recognizable spill-over effects for the department. The doctoral program, which was being redesigned at the same time that CAPP came into existence, has moved toward a cohort approach and will include a focus on field-based internships that are appropriate to the preparation of superintendents and other central-office administrators. In fact, at least one mentor has applied for admissions to the doctoral program as a result of her experience in CAPP and her understanding that the doctoral program is becoming more practitioner oriented. In addition, another preparation program, at Central Connecticut University, has taken note of the changes being made at the University of Connecticut by adding the requirement of an internship to its program.

ONGOING ISSUES

The University of Connecticut has managed to overcome a number of early problems and has been able to continue the growth and to improve the quality of its innovative leadership preparation program. As might be expected at this early stage, there are many things that can still be pursued to further improve the program. In fact, some of the following suggestions are already being considered by the coordinator and the Educational Leadership Department.

Academic Program

The program is undergoing major changes, including a shift from courses toward the inclusion of modules; the teaming of faculty members with leading practitioners to enrich students' learnings; inclusion of practical experiences in courses, such as case studies, role-playing opportunities, simulations, and assignments that require diagnoses of site-based situations. However, there are other changes that might also need to be considered.

First, to model the kinds of learning environments that cohort members will be expected to lead, some faculty may need to modify their traditional approaches to course management. In this regard, although some courses are presented in a fashion that promotes interactive learning, team activities, and critical thinking, others are more representative of traditional programs wherein professors decide on course content, how it will be delivered, what students will do to master the materials, and how they will be evaluated in their effort. Students in educational administration programs are mature learners. In fact, they are instructors themselves in other settings, and they are preparing to take on proactive leadership roles. Every effort should be made to provide learning experiences that reflect these facts.

Second, although it is too early to make judgments about educational modules, introducing modules midway through the program is a questionable step. If modules are appropriate, and they probably are, it makes better sense to introduce them at the outset of the program, so that students become acquainted with this approach immediately. In fact, some early program courses are already organized in a number of categorical blocks and often call for different instructors to present specific material. Modifying such courses to fit the modular approach would not be difficult.

Third, the program promotes cohort development, much like other Danforth programs across the country. Students place a high value on this program aspect, both for the support they receive from peers and for the learning and networking they gain from participating in the cohort. The cohort concept can be further enriched by inclusion of a retreat, near the beginning of the program, that emphasizes team building and group development. It can also be enhanced by more frequent reflective seminars, which are more likely to lead to peer sharing than are formal classes that are guided by professors with established objectives, course content, and class management routines. Finally, although there is much value in having mentors attend reflective seminars, limiting their participation (e.g., setting expectations for mentors' roles, delaying their involvement until a few sessions have been experienced so students become accustomed to participating more fully, and reserving some part of the reflective seminar time exclusively for cohort interactions) may help promote cohort development.

Fourth, the school/community project, leadership project, and portfolio activities are all effective means of emphasizing the leadership aspect of running schools. Bringing these activities together in a synthesizing exercise at the conclusion of the program could be an enriching experience for students. The leadership activity could provide the organizational foundation of the exercise. For example, students might make oral presentations of their leadership projects, incorporating a presentation and summarization of their total portfolio as supportive evidence. This presentation might be done before a panel of educational leaders, both as a rite of passage and as an opportunity to network with established leaders.

Recruitment and Admissions

The rapid increase in qualified applicants to CAPP is indicative of major improvements already in place regarding recruitment and admissions. Five suggestions are offered to further improve this situation. First, there is still a wide disparity in the ways that school districts go about recruiting and screening candidates. Some devote much energy to this activity, purposefully encouraging staff members with potential for leadership to consider the program and then helping them move through the nomination process. Others treat the activity with less intensity, simply distributing announcements of the program's availability. It would be beneficial for the coordinator to develop a written statement of expectations for school districts' roles in this activity and to make frequent contact with key district leaders to help socialize them to expectations.

Second, consistent language that refers to the districts' role as being nomination, rather than selection, is important. Because this distinction is not always clear, problems may arise in the future. However it chooses to do so, selection remains a prerogative of the department.

Third, orientation sessions sponsored by the department during the winter months preceding admission of a new cohort should be considered. Such sessions could reduce the disparity in information that interested individuals now receive from the many well-intended, but not always fully knowledgeable, school-district administrators who initially suggest their participation in the program. Sessions would also allow members of the current cohort to share perceptions about the program from a participant point of view, enabling potential candidates to get a better sense of the efforts required and the outcomes that can be anticipated.

Fourth, admissions criteria and evidence are rather traditional, with the exception of an interview that emphasizes candidates' educational beliefs and career goal focus. The faculty may want to consider the addition of a process, such as a behaviorally anchored activity, that provides evidence of candidates' leadership potential.

Fifth, purposeful recruitment of minorities is recognized as an important consideration. For example, the coordinator approached the Hartford School District prior to CAPP II and was successful in gaining that district's cooperation by emphasizing the need to bring ethnic and racial minorities into the program. In fact, because of the focus on minorities, the district was able to use its affirmative-action funds to support candidates' release time. Except for this case, however, candidate identification has been left to the districts, without much guidance toward this objective. Given the growing proportion of the school-age minority population in the state, this will become an increasingly important consideration.

Internships

The original internship configuration was modified in order to save the program from going out of business. Although this was appropriate at the time, it is necessary for the faculty to explore any and all means of strengthening the current configuration.

First, efforts should be made to increase the portion of the 90 days of clinical experiences accomplished during the regular academic year, when student groups are in school. In this regard, the planners may want to consider pressing school districts to increase incrementally their release-time commitment as the state's economy begins to recover; encouraging students to make more efforts to find additional school-year days through use of holidays, leave time, and even making financial contributions to cover substitute costs for release time as members of CAPP I did; and continuing to approach the state's department of education to become a resource partner, particularly given that the state will soon require an internship of all administrative certification applicants.

Second, many cohort members would benefit by increased guidance in establishing internship goals and activities. At present, the department provides a handbook with a suggested set of activities and encourages cohort members to focus on learning areas they think they need most when identifying and discussing clinical experience objectives with their mentors. However, at the outset of the program, new cohort members may not have sufficient knowledge to be able to make wise decisions about use of internship time. Similarly, as they begin to identify activities at their internship sites, students may require more written information about the assumptions and regarding educational change and the role of leaders in schools that guide the program.

The coordinator may want to consider upgrading the handbook to include a statement of beliefs and a set of expected categories of experiences (e.g., community relations, staff development, budgeting, and discipline) in which interns should participate. This could provide a universal basis for negotiating learning experiences, while still leaving room for consideration of individuals' unique learning needs. It could also provide the basis for renegotiating objectives in the second year, when mentors and interns try to sort out what has and what has not yet been accomplished as they establish learning priorities for that year.

Third, mentoring is an important aspect of the program. In fact, most interns speak of the relationship with their mentors with great enthusiasm. To further improve this dynamic, the faculty should consider putting more effort into the training of mentors (e.g., what is expected in the role, coaching strategies, sequencing interns' activities in ways that move from shadowing to responsibility for activities, and ways of integrating the program's academic content with activities in the field). It may be possible to develop a system that allows mentors to interview cohort members seeking internships rather than limiting placement to the coordinator's judgment, so that mentors and interns can have a say about the situation, and the interpersonal "chemistry" of mentoring can be more fully considered. The faculty could explain the mentors' role during the interns' summer activities so that more effective, meaningful, and positive learning experiences could be planned. Finally, the faculty might consider the creation of a system of mentor evaluation so that supportive and corrective feedback can be provided to enhance these educational leaders' mentoring abilities.

Fourth, field supervision is an important link in the process. At present, full-time faculty members are responsible for this activity. As might be expected, the results are mixed, depending on faculty members' knowledge of school dynamics and the time they have to attend to this important task. If faculty continue to participate as field supervisors, they should receive adequate training and appropriate load credit. However, it might be wiser to reserve necessary resources to hire and train outstanding K-12 administrators to manage this function. Such high-repute field leaders would be viewed more legitimately by mentors and would also probably be more sensitive to the learning needs of interns.

Fifth, interns report that reflective seminars are critically important to them, both for the opportunities provided to process observations and interactions at school sites, and for the chance to interact openly with other cohort members. Reflective seminars presently meet once a month, starting in the second semester of the program. Only one credit is granted for this and the internship activity, and attendance at seminars is not required. It might be beneficial to reconfigure the program's credits, increase the frequency of reflective seminar meetings to enhance cohort members' learning, and require attendance.

Sixth, at present, interns' home-site principals are not involved in the program in any respect. As a result, they often view their staff members' absences while interning as a high cost to their own schools. Often, they know little about the program beyond the difficulties it creates for their schools. Nor do they have a sense of how they might compound the learnings of their staff members. For example, they could be encouraged to act as secondary mentors by involving cohort members in home-site leadership activities. The department might reap positive results by creating systems that involve these principals and help them to see the potential benefit for their own sites, in the form of an increased leadership capacity if their staff members remain as teacher-leaders.

Placement

CAPP has only four graduates thus far, so it is too early to make judgments about placement. However, given the negative budget situation that exists in many school systems, as well as the high compensation level for leadership positions, which tends to attract many qualified candidates from the entire New England region, as well as New York and New Jersey, planners may need to think of ways to help graduates compete in this difficult marketplace. As one district leader noted, the department may need to encourage school districts to identify "quasi-administrative" positions for CAPP graduates to provide them with leadership titles for their résumés and may need to involve them in activities that may make a difference when potential hiring districts are reviewing candidates' folders. Such titles as coordinator of reading or coordinator of curriculum in a school may be helpful in this regard.

Certainly as the number of graduates increases, the coordinator will need to maintain records of the positions that graduates hold so that the department has some sense of placement trends. Also, over time, as CAPP graduates move into responsible positions, they can be asked to provide networking help to later cohort members.

Financing

The program is presently underfinanced, both in the area of release time for internship activities and in the area of program management. Ways of improving the release-time situation have already been explored. Regarding program management, greater efforts will have to be made to support this area, particularly as the department begins to move toward admissions of cohorts on an annual basis, which means that the coordinator will be coping with twice the number of students and cohorts in two different developmental stages at any given time.

If the School of Education expects to maintain and expand the program, it clearly must increase the resources it puts into the program, to provide adequate release time for the coordinator and to provide the secretarial and field supervision help that are so desperately needed.

A source of funds that should be explored may be through the Continuing Education Division. Currently, students pay tuition for up to six credits of internship for each of two summers, a process that is administered through the Continuing Education Division. It is possible that an understanding can be reached whereby most of these tuition dollars are returned to the department for management of the program, particularly since the effort required of the Continuing Education Division is limited to registration and recording grades. A similar argument can also be made for some of the tuition dollars that go through regular university channels, based on the fact that facilities and supervision are provided outside the university.

Partnering

Relations are good and improving between department faculty and participating school-district leaders. However, the partnership is far from equal. The coordinator consults regularly with school leaders, but typically on a one-to-one basis, which appears to be the tradition for the department. A true partnership that equally values all partners' inputs and promotes initiative-taking on the part of district leaders may require more formal structures, more opportunities to meet as groups, and a clear set of purposes and prerogatives for such gatherings. A good starting place might be the creation of an overall advisory committee from among the many site-based administrators who have become mentors and from district-level leaders who have been active partners. Subsequently, as the network of field-based partners grows, other purpose-limited partnership committees can be formed (e.g., for overall program guidance, curriculum development, and internship management).

Coordination

The coordination of the program is strong. The current coordinator, who is viewed positively by district and site-based leaders, has been able to get interested parties to agree to necessary program changes and has the insights that are necessary to increase the viability of the program. Her own advanced training and rich experience as a principal, as well as her extraordinary energy and enthusiasm, combine to make her the ideal person to coordinate CAPP.

What is now required is a support system that will enable her to function effectively. As noted, this requires the university and the school to commit resources that are necessary for program management. It also requires a clear understanding of the value of the effort that is being made, particularly as faculty load is considered and as retention and tenure decisions are made. The role of coordinating CAPP is significantly different from traditional expectations for faculty productivity. This difference has to be understood and supported if the coordinator is expected to continue making the program a high-priority activity. Understanding and modification of expectations at both the department's and the dean's levels will be required.

Finally, consistent and formal efforts must be made to involve other educational administration faculty members in coordinating activities. This can help the coordinator with a difficult task. Even more important, it is a way of maintaining faculty understanding and responsiveness to the changing curricular needs that such a program requires and a way of keeping them closer to what is actually happening in schools. Without such involvement, it is likely that faculty members will turn their attention away from the program over time and toward other emerging group and individual priorities.

In Closing

The University of Connecticut represents a situation that is likely to occur at many other universities that attempt to introduce similar program changes. It is a daunting task to create such significant changes, particularly in settings that are relatively stable, where budgetary constraints prevail, and there is little existing motivation to take the risks that are required. In such a situation, the courage to stay the course is a vitally important ingredient, as is the willingness to negotiate and compromise to gain necessary support, but in ways that ensure that the integrity of the effort is maintained.

The Pied Piper Creates a Vision

California State University at Fresno

California State University at Fresno (CSUF) began planning for its Danforth program in 1990 and enrolled its first cohort during the summer of 1991. Since that time, one cohort group has completed the program (December 1991), a second cohort group is approximately one half through the program (a second group finished in December of 1992), and a third group began the program in January of 1992.

Fresno would not be the place one might expect to have taken a leading role in the development of alternative educational leadership program designs. In fact, the few faculty interested in administrator preparation were quite content to maintain the university's rather traditional preparation program. The initiative required to rally the faculty and area educational leaders to create and operate an alternative program design can be traced to one individual. This "pied piper," as he is referred to by those who joined him in the effort, is a faculty member who recently joined the university after helping to design a Danforth program at another university. His vision, salesmanship, and tenacity won over others.

This chapter summarizes the learnings gained in this Danforth program. After setting the scene with some information about the region, the university, and the education administration unit, the program is described in some detail. This description is followed by an analysis of key dynamics that have had impact on the program.

The Setting

CSUF lies at the heart of one of the nation's richest agricultural areas, the Central Valley of California. Metropolitan Fresno, which is growing rapidly, has a population of 635,000, 318,000 of whom reside within the Fresno city limits.

CSUF, which is part of the California State University system, began in 1911 as a normal school, with 150 students. In the past 80 years, it has been transformed into a comprehensive institution of higher learning, with nearly 20,000 registered students, offering graduate programs in 42 different areas. There are more than 2,000 graduate students and about 450 master's degrees are awarded annually. A cooperative doctoral program between CSUF and four University of California campuses has recently been approved.

The population served by the Educational Administration Program at CSUF can be described as challenging. Because the Central Valley has some of the most reasonable housing costs in California, it attracts many families of lower socioeconomic status, including many farm workers and, recently, immigrants from various parts of the world. More than 70 different languages are spoken in the valley (18.2% of the students in Fresno County are listed as having "limited English proficiency"). More than 30% of the children in school receive Aid for Families with Dependent Children support and the local social services agency reports that approximately 20% of area families are eligible for some form of assistance. Not surprisingly, the school dropout rate in the area is about 20%, with the city system reporting rates of more than 30%. Similarly, test results show an unusually high percentage of students scoring in the lowest quartile on statewide tests.

Readiness for Change

Prior to initiating the Danforth-related field-based program, the Educational Administration Program (which is housed in the School of Education and Human Development's Department of Educational Research, Administration, and Foundations) offered a relatively traditional preparation program with course titles that include leadership, supervision, law, community relations, and finance. The quality and intensity of field experiences varied widely.

The faculty consists of four tenure-track members, as well as several short-term and adjunct faculty members. There has been a major turnover in faculty recently. Of the tenure-track group, the most senior member has been at CSUF for only 6 years. The coordinator of the Danforth program, who had the benefit of being a Danforth program coordinator at another institution, has been at Fresno for less than 4 years. Two others have been on faculty for less than 2 years.

Area superintendents have expressed a concern about the need to focus on leadership development. They note that the rapidly changing and ever-more-diverse population of the valley requires that tomorrow's educational leaders include more members of ethnic and racial minority groups. These leaders, regardless of their own ethnic and racial origin, need increased sensitivity to and understanding of multicultural realities. Further, they must be able to provide instructional leadership to meet diverse student needs. These superintendents have also been concerned about insufficient numbers of high-quality individuals available locally to meet these needs. For example, over the past 7 years, one school district has felt it necessary to hire all of its administrators from outside the local area.

A basic factor in the development of readiness has been the strong partnership between the educational administration faculty and superintendents in the area, particularly those from medium- to small-sized school districts. The program coordinator has worked with these superintendents to identify a common set of purposes that focus on identifying and preparing area educators for leadership roles. The coordinator has regularly attended superintendents' meetings, listened to their concerns about the university's preparation program, and shared his concern about the valley's changing demographics and their implications for educational leadership.

In response to these interactions, several high-reputation superintendents have encouraged their peers to join them in partnership with the university to create and support the Danforth program.

The partnership has grown over the past 2 years to include an advisory committee composed of all superintendents who have placed students in the program. This committee meets approximately every 6 months to give overall advice and feedback. A steering committee of five or six superintendents provides more frequent feedback and advice. In fact, steering committee members frequently meet with the coordinator over lunch or dinner to plan cooperatively. They also serve on curriculum-writing teams and are actively engaged with the program coordinator in developing program-design changes.

Description of the Program

The intent of the Danforth program is to adapt the CSUF educational-administration program in ways that lead to better preparation of leaders for area schools. Specifically, the effort is intended to concentrate on providing leadership that will have a positive impact on the educational performance of the diverse student group that constitutes the area's school population. Thus the program is intended to emphasize educational leadership within a multicultural context.

ACADEMIC CONTENT AND DELIVERY

The structure and content of the Danforth program differs significantly from the currently institutionalized program, which, like many others across the country, is composed of traditional courses that can be taken in any order that students prefer. Fieldwork is required, but students' experiences vary widely in length, intensity, and quality of supervision. The Danforth program, which the faculty has agreed will replace the existing program if the university approves this change, includes the following academic elements:

1. Students enroll in a sequenced set of academic experiences, two courses per semester, over an 18-month period of time (including summers). The following courses are taken as a cohort group:

Semester One:	Advanced Educational Psychology/Management
Semester Two:	Curriculum/Leadership
Semester Three:	Research Methods/Supervision
Semester Four:	Project/Site-Based Leadership

2. Emphasis is on hands-on, high involvement, participative learning in seminars. This is intended to help students gain a better understanding of educational organizations and their own orientation toward educational leadership.

3. Besides regular courses, workshops are designed around topics of interest to the students. For example, recent topics have included mentor-protégé relationships, psychology of the culturally distinct learner, curriculum-driven schools, classroom supervision, and site-based leadership. These 1-day or more workshops, which are taken for academic credit, reduce the number of hours given over to the on-campus seminars just identified.

4. There is high involvement by area superintendents in the design of academic experiences and the basic approach to field site activities. This includes an ongoing advisory committee, a steering committee, and curriculum-writing teams, which bring together administrators and faculty members.

STUDENTS

Students in the program (18 in the first cohort, 24 in the second, and 27 in the third) are initially identified by their district superintendents. This recruitment through leader sponsorship has resulted in the identification of area educators who are viewed as individuals with high potential for leadership.

Those who accept their superintendent's invitation then apply to the faculty for admission. The admissions process is much like the process employed at other institutions. It includes the filing of transcripts, GRE scores, and recommendations.

Students in the first and second cohorts were already in some form of administrative position or were placed in one just prior to entering the program. These positions include program specialists and learning coordinators, as well as assistant principals. Due in part at least to the aforementioned fiscal constraints, only 5 of the students in the third cohort are presently in administrative positions, while the other 22 are classroom-based teachers. Most of these candidates, however, are from year-round schools. They will move into administrative fieldwork positions full-time while they are "off track" and free from teaching responsibilities.

Given the emphasis on multiculturalism, efforts have been made to promote diversity within the cohort groups. Initially, this did occur. In the first cohort, 33% were male and 44% were of an ethnic or racial minority (8 Hispanic-Americans and 1 Asian-American). For the second cohort, males constituted 46% of the group and 46% were ethnic or racial minorities (9 Hispanic-Americans, 1 African-American, and 1 Asian-American). However, the superintendent sponsorship system makes it difficult to control the demographic mix adequately. As a result, there has been a major change in the third cohort, which is less than 19% male and 15% ethnic or racial minority (3 Hispanic-Americans and 1 Native American).

The first cohort just completed its program in December of 1991, so it is premature to make strong conclusions about placement. However, it is relevant to note that 12 of the 18 educators in that group currently hold administrative appointments—4 as principals. Only 2 of the 12 were in such positions prior to their enrollment, so the program has already led to career shifts for more than half of the participants. It should be noted that this has occurred in an environment where there are many more aspirants than openings for administrative appointments.

INTERNSHIPS

Clinical experiences occur during the second and third semesters of the program. The second clinical experience can be delayed one or two semesters if the student's work schedule requires such a delay.

The first and second cohorts have been able to experience more than 1500 hours of clinical experiences because they have been assigned, full- or half-time, to administrative positions during their involvement in the program. Internship experiences include opportunities to observe or shadow a site administrator, and to take on administrative responsibilities that are planned and agreed on by the field supervisor, site supervisor, and the intern.

A guidebook containing a set of required competencies is employed to establish goals and activities. It is also used in the pre-post-evaluation process. During the second semester, interns are required to seek opportunities to spend part of their time with an administrator at a different school level than the one to which they were initially assigned. Field supervisors visit interns' sites about twice a semester.

There are no formally designed reflective seminars. However, during academic seminars and specialized workshops, students have many opportunities to reflect on their experiences.

Interns are assigned to mentors, often the superintendents who have sponsored their involvement. In some cases, a true mentoring relationship developed, but more often, the bonding that takes place between the site supervisor and the intern has led to the most meaningful mentoring relationships. In addition, as the first cohort has completed the program and moved into administrative positions, members of the second and third cohort frequently seek out these individuals as mentors. In fact, at times, the coordinator asks an alumnus of the program to act as a mentor if it is thought that this can be of help to a particular intern.

COORDINATION

The program at Fresno has been coordinated by one faculty member since its inception. His experience included originating a program at a Danforth-related institution prior to coming to Fresno. In addition to this experience, his exceptional networking abilities enabled him to create a group of superintendents who joined him as partners and sponsors of the program.

In addition to coordination responsibilities, he also teaches courses and is head of the academic unit. It is only because of his high energy and dedication to the program that the many complex activities associated with the endeavor are completed. It would not be surprising if he eventually grows weary of the intensive and fast pace required to keep all the pieces together. Equally important, as long as he remains the sole overseer of the program, other faculty members will not feel responsible for its continuation.

FINANCIAL ARRANGEMENTS

The program has been funded from multiple sources—the foundation, students, and school districts. The coordinator asked for and received a second and third year of funding from the Danforth Foundation, thus ensuring the availability of flexible start-up funds for an extended period of time.

Students are responsible for paying tuition and fees for the program. More important, students in the first and second cohorts who did not already hold administrative positions were released from their ongoing duties full- or half-time by their school districts to be part of the Danforth program. This fiscal commitment, which required replacement costs for area school systems of about $750,000 for the first cohort and $1,250,000 for the second cohort, permitted students to focus exclusively on their field- and campus-based learnings.

The burdens encountered as a result of the recessionary situation in California have caused area school-district leaders to reduce severely their current financial commitment to the program. Students in the third cohort receive only limited financial support from their school districts; in most situations, this support amounts to funding for substitutes for approximately 8 to 12 workshop days. As is noted later herein, there are many ramifications of this fiscal situation, including the length and timing of field experiences, as well as the extent to which students are able to focus on their learnings.

To respond to fiscal realities, the program is moving toward a more flexible approach. Four options have been identified: full-time district support, half-time district support, off-track fieldwork experiences for those in year-round schools, and summer internships for those in non-year-round school sites. Almost half of the schools in the Fresno area are year-round, so there are plentiful opportunities for summer internships.

Analysis

The Danforth program initiative has had a powerful impact on the preparation of educational leaders in the Central Valley, and it has accomplished this in an extraordinarily short period of time. Beneficial payoffs are clearly identifiable for the individuals involved, as well as for the institutions they serve.

BENEFICIAL PAYOFFS

Payoffs for Students

Twelve of the 18 members of the first cohort group are currently in administrative positions. These individuals have made significant career changes. The sponsorship system and the high selectivity of candidates admitted to the Danforth program appears to have had a positive impact on the willingness of superintendents to hire graduates of the CSUF program.

Equally important, cohort members report a sense of enthusiasm about the program effects. In particular, they feel positive about the following:

- Being involved in a cohort composed of exceptional individuals
- Participating in a sequenced set of hands-on, highly interactive learning experiences that have direct application to their world of work
- The high quality of their relationships with university faculty members who are committed to the improvement of educational leadership in the valley
- Having the opportunity to take on real responsibilities in administrative situations as interns
- The sponsorship they receive from their superintendents and site supervisors

Such factors combine to create a transformational experience. That is, being treated as adults and challenged to grow, they are becoming the best they can be. In this regard, it is interesting to contrast the growth-stage differences observable in the three cohort groups. Members of the group that has just finished appear confident and excited about entering the administrative ranks and have established extensive networks among themselves and with many of the area's educational leaders. Members of the second cohort, midway through the experience, began to take on the mental maps that administrators must have in order to understand and improve the complex organizations that they lead. They are growing together as a group in ways that hold promise for the future. The third cohort, when in the program for less than 2 months, was still not clear about the program or about the cohort members' own sense of purpose in joining it.

In short, much more than content and skill learning seems to take place in this highly intensive preparation program. Participants report personal beliefs about the impact of the program such as the following: more confidence about their ability to handle administrative responsibilities; a clearer understanding of the impact of personal leadership styles on others; the ability to communicate better; different perceptions of administrators and the realities of their work roles; the need to listen to both sides and not react immediately; the development of an extensive network of resource people; a feeling of self-esteem as a result of being sponsored by the superintendent; a chance to deal with leadership realities "up front" before having to perform in a permanent position; a chance to give gifts back to the district in the form of projects completed; a chance to work with exceptional educational leaders and to be mentored as learning occurs; and the personal growth that comes out of such an intensive and challenging program.

Payoffs for Site Supervisors

In most cases, site supervisors were identified and selected by superintendents, sometimes because of leadership qualities and other times because of particular district-based needs and learning opportunities available at the school site. Those who took on site-supervision activities frequently did not volunteer for this assignment. Even though they had not chosen to become involved in the program, site supervisors report with great frequency the feeling that they have gained at least as much as their interns. Among these gains are the following:

- Having a chance to work with exemplary individuals who challenge them to do their best
- Insights and feedback from interns about the schools they run
- The positive effects on the school of the projects that interns initiate and conduct
- A chance to share their expertise
- An opportunity to reflect on why they lead as they do rather than just operating by instinct
- Getting a chance to be updated about what is going on in educational administration
- The chance to have regular contacts with university personnel
- The general sense of self-renewal that is gained by participating in this challenging endeavor

The point is that site supervisors receive an opportunity for professional development through their involvement with the Danforth program. Given time and financial constraints, for many, this is an opportunity that would otherwise not be available. This is an important, if indirect, program payoff. Site supervisors are often in midcareer as educational leaders. They have much to offer or they would not have survived at that level. However, they need opportunities to continue their own professional development if they are to remain enthused and have the skills to lead in challenging places and times.

Payoffs for School Districts

The interns' and site supervisors' gains are, of course, also gains to the district. An expanding leadership pool creates the energy and potential for the districts to respond to the needs of their students and communities. Beyond this fact, there are also other payoffs. Superintendents report that they believe that problems dealt with at school sites will be less likely to land on their desks in the future. This gives them more confidence in their administrative team and, equally important, frees them to focus on overall system management and long-term planning activities.

In addition, superintendents note that their participation on the advisory committee and the steering committee has given them much-needed opportunities to converse with their peers from other school districts. This emerging network of area superintendents, based on a cooperative effort, rather than the competitive situations in which they frequently find themselves (i.e., fighting for their district's "fair share" of fiscal and material resources), has begun to change the way they relate to one another. In fact, they are beginning to think of themselves as a group of educators who are concerned about the overall well-being of students and communities throughout the valley, rather than the more parochial perspective of being the champions of their particular district's needs.

In the process, they are also beginning to believe in the university's concern and ability to help in meeting the needs of the valley's school districts. The positive results accruing from partnerships with the Danforth program appear to be spreading to other university and school-district cooperative efforts. For example, a new program called SURCOL (School and University Research Collaborative) promotes research efforts that are responsive to school-district-identified problem areas and that include professionals from the field and from the university as research team members. Likewise, the educational administration faculty has established an administrative-assessment center on campus, in cooperation with the National Association of Elementary School Principals. The superintendents involved with the Danforth program, seeing much potential for assessment of Danforth scholars and for professional development of their own administrative teams, are participating in planning for the center.

Payoffs for University/College/Educational
Administration Unit

As is true of most universities, CSUF recognizes that it needs to expand its ability to be of service to the local community. This is particularly true in a structure such as the University of California system, where students who attend institutions such as CSUF come from the surrounding population center. Good public relations are vital in such a situation, as is the need to promote excellence in education so that students arrive at the university with a solid foundation for academic success. The president of CSUF, acknowledging this reality, has publicly endorsed the Danforth program and has written a strong statement to the educational administration faculty, encouraging its support of the program. This endorsement has sent a clear message to the faculty, indicating that the university believes that such outreach efforts as the Danforth program are important to the well-being of the institution. The message also provides a special opportunity for the faculty to seek favorable conditions for rewards such as tenure as they take up the challenge.

The School of Education and Human Development, which is purposefully reaching out to collaborate collegially with its local clientele, is gradually recognizing that the Danforth program provides a useful model for the achievement of this goal. Both the dean and the associate dean noted that cooperative developments emerging from the Danforth program will be useful to the entire school as it seeks to improve and broaden its partnerships with the area's school systems.

At the department and unit level, change has been difficult. After all, the Danforth program represents a threat to the psychic energy and investment of those who have helped to create the current program. That program is well-established and is fairly reflective of programs at similar institutions across the country. It is taking time for the faculty to become convinced regarding the value of the Danforth experiment and, equally important, to have the opportunity to grieve and let go of the established program. However, much to their credit, this transition is occurring. The faculty has recommended that the Danforth program become the only department route to certification. This significant change was put in place as of the summer of 1992.

Over time, the faculty will have regular opportunities to become involved with innovations created through the Danforth program. They will be teaching courses that have been newly approved by the department, and they will be supervising interns. Faculty members will have more opportunities to interact and collaborate collegially with the area's educational leaders and to identify projects that can enrich their courses and expand their opportunities to write about field-based issues.

In addition to obvious benefits that have occurred, there are also some problems that must be addressed if the program is to meet desired objectives. These issues, which are to be expected when changes of this magnitude are implemented, can be addressed by thoughtful and creative planning.

Academic Program

There are four program-related issues that will need to be addressed. First, the program has been established in order to serve a culturally diverse population. However, multiculturalism as a concept is not as well-integrated into the program as it might be. There are explorations of multicultural dynamics that students bring from field-site experiences, but there is little to indicate that issues associated with multicultural education are being purposefully designed as part of the program delivery scheme, either in academic seminars or in field-site experiences. Multiculturalism is an important aspect of the program, given the environment that surrounds the university. The faculty and the advisory group may want to explore ways of enhancing this program element.

Second, the concept of instructional leadership does not appear to have been developed fully. There is an emphasis on the principal's role as instructional leader, rather than as plant manager, but a broader concept of leadership is probably necessary. Leadership needs to be viewed as a function, rather than as a person. This is appropriate, given the adult community that these students will eventually facilitate and given the emphasis on site-based and participative management that are in vogue in school districts. Although there is much programmatic movement in this direction, it appears that there is still room for the faculty and their field-based partners to expand this important concept.

Third, all faculty members will be teaching in the program once it becomes the unit's single approach. Serious staff-development efforts will be required to ensure that the richness of courses designed for the Danforth program will continue. As an illustration, teaching styles may have to be modified to emphasize hands-on activities, high participation, and opportunities for reflection about site-based experiences.

Finally, institutionalization will have a direct effect on the way students are grouped for instructional purposes. CSUF is a public institution, which means that it would be hard pressed to deny admission to "walk-in" students if they meet admissions criteria. Therefore, as the Danforth program becomes the only CSUF program, those students who are sponsored by their superintendents will be attending classes with nonsponsored students. This mix may present problems if the two groups are different in commitment, ability, and experience. Because it will significantly reduce the opportunity for interactions among the sponsored group, it can also dilute the impact of the cohort concept, which has been identified as such a powerful element of the program. Further, classes may be larger, which will also make it more difficult to maintain an interactive and participative environment. These problems will need to be resolved if the strengths of the program are to be retained.

Recruitment and Admissions

Although students in the first and second cohorts are representative of the valley's minority groups and are fairly well balanced by gender, the third group does not reflect the general population base of the area. Representativeness may be difficult to maintain as long as selection is left exclusively to the sponsorship of school district superintendents. Perhaps arrangement can be established by which demographic data of nominees are reviewed against the criteria of gender and multicultural diversity prior to final selections being made.

Internships

Three issues relate to the internship aspect of the program. First, the Danforth effort at CSUF has been in place for more than 2 years. The faculty is substituting the in-place program with the newer Danforth program model. However, there appear to be major consequences associated with that acceptance. In particular, the faculty has established a minimum of 150 clinical internship hours, which is a significant drop from the average of 1500 hours experienced by the first and second cohorts (the 1500-hour expectation is about three times that of other Danforth programs and more like six to eight times the norm of most other institutions). Because the extent of field-site experiences has been such an important element in the students' programs, the compromise that the faculty is making may cause the loss of one of the most important elements in the program's success.

Second, if the third cohort is indicative of things to come, classroom-based teachers are likely to constitute the largest proportion of students who will enter the program. This may be occurring because financially strapped districts are having difficulty creating administrative roles for interns. Whatever the cause, this demographic change has tremendous implications. Members of the third cohort are less experienced, have not established the "mental maps" required of successful administrators, and are constrained in their ability to secure meaningful field-site administrative experiences. Somehow, this problem will have to be addressed in ways beyond limiting site-based experiences to summers or other off-track opportunities.

Finally, the decision has been made that faculty will act as field supervisors of students who are sponsored by their superintendents. The faculty will have to be sensitized to program objectives, operational expectations for field supervision, and role modifications they will encounter as they work with these students.

Placement

Thus far, program graduates have been quite successful in gaining placement as administrators. Both the sponsorship system and the development of meaningful field-based experiences are positive program elements that make this possible. These advantages are no longer in place. The third cohort, and probably the cohorts of the future, will have less district support in the form of release time, and members will come from the ranks of teachers more than of individuals already in quasi-administrative roles. Serious consideration will have to be given to these realities, and alternative approaches may need to be developed if the placement record that has been achieved is going to continue.

Financing

As noted, recessionary pressures have caused a major shift in the financing of the program. The third cohort group is receiving only minor financial help from the districts. If the financial constraints they presently face persist, this is likely to become the norm. If it does, it will threaten the ability of faculty and field leaders to provide candidates with the time-on-task and meaningful administrative experiences they must have to build confidence and skills required for leadership positions.

Equally worrisome is the fact that the university has yet to make an ongoing commitment to provide the resources necessary to support the university president's stated commitment to nurture the program. Minimally, this will require a staff person who can monitor activities and respond to requests for information, a secretary who can serve the growing needs of the program and keep the paperwork in order, and space in which these individuals can function. Without such support, the program will remain the sole responsibility of the director (who is also program coordinator for the educational administration unit!), an unrealistic expectation that may lead to loss of enthusiasm for continuing this complex and time-consuming effort.

Partnering

Maintaining the momentum that has been established in the partnership between the university and the field is of vital importance. It will have an impact on expansion of purposes beyond the current Danforth program effort, as well as on meaningful site experiences for students and on support—both fiscal and symbolic—for those selected to be in the program. As leaders come and go, there will have to be efforts to socialize and bring along the next generation of these individuals, who will be asked to make continuing efforts to find resources and to network with the university during the hard times that may be ahead. Efforts to formalize the partnership (e.g., with rotating slots on the steering committee, regular meetings with the faculty as well as the coordinator, and clarification of expectations) may be in order.

Coordination

Superintendents refer to the Danforth program coordinator as the "Pied Piper." By this, they mean that they recognize that such significant programmatic changes as the Danforth program require a champion with the vision and energy to put necessary elements in place. However, it is also a fact that as long as such efforts remain the personal domain of one or two individuals, such efforts are not likely to be embedded and institutionalized within the system. Beyond an injection of resources to provide staff, space, and material support needs, if the program is to persist, the coordinator needs the understanding and involvement of the faculty.

In Closing

The experience at the California State University at Fresno demonstrates how powerful one individual can be, who has the vision, skill, and tenacity to bring about important changes in preparation programs for educational leaders. The program has already trained a large number of potential leaders for the Central Valley, and it has now become the single program approach of the university. This is an impressive change, particularly in the short time that the effort has been in place.

A Prize Winner Improves

University of Washington

The University of Washington, a member of Danforth's second cycle, is in its fifth year of the new program. The university initiated its experimental program and launched its first cohort in the summer of 1988, the same year that its regular program won an Outstanding Program Award from the American Association of School Administrators.

The recognition granted by that association suggests that the Educational Leadership and Policy Studies Area of the University of Washington's College of Education is not a latecomer to programmatic review and improvement. The fact that a new program approach was being tested at the same time that this recognition was being received is also important. It indicates that the area was fully aware that it must give continuous attention to program change, and improvement must be a priority for it to have a positive impact on the preparation of educational leaders.

This chapter summarizes the Washington Danforth program, which, in the fall of 1992, became the area's only certification program for principal preparation. After setting the scene, the program is described and critiqued. Finally, lessons that may be of help to other universities are shared.

The Setting

The state of Washington is growing rapidly in population. There are 4.8 million people in the state, up sharply from 4.1 million in 1987. The school-age population reached 817,000 in 1970, before declining, but it has since rebounded and is on an upward growth curve, reaching 888,000 in 1991.

The counties that compose the Puget Sound area, which surrounds the University of Washington, make up the fastest-growing area of the state, with a population of approximately 2.8 million and an expanding economic base, as opposed to the recessionary climate that predominates in other areas of the state. About one quarter of the Puget Sound population resides in the cities of Seattle and Tacoma.

The growth in the region's population is directly related to its robust economy and the seemingly endless need for highly trained and specially skilled personnel, who simply cannot be trained in sufficient numbers locally. The regional economy is dominated by several high-technology industries, including airplane manufacturing (Boeing), which has plateaued; biotechnologies, which is growing; and software development (Microsoft), which is booming. Washington is also the largest trading state in the nation, due mainly to its geographical proximity to the Pacific Rim.

The positive economy is also affecting inter-school-district population shifts. For example, housing prices in Seattle have been driven up to the point that lower-income families are seeking housing in first-ring suburbs. This significantly affects school-district populations—downward in Seattle and upward in adjacent communities. There is also a small rural population at the outer fringes of the mountains and on the islands.

Over the past 20 years, the racial and ethnic minority population of the Puget Sound area grew from about 80,000 to more than 228,000. It has also changed in composition, with large increases in the Hispanic-American and Asian-American populations, and it has expanded from urban areas into the closely surrounding suburbs (e.g., Seattle has a 57% racial and ethnic-minority population in its schools, while neighboring Bellevue has 21%, and more distant Northshore has only 8%, almost all of whom are Asian-Americans). Overall, 44% of the area's ethnic and racial minorities now reside in suburban communities.

The Puget Sound area includes school districts varying from core area urban centers to rural mountain and island towns. The 25 largest school districts had a student population of approximately 380,000 in 1991, down by about 110,00 since the 1960s, when the student population peaked. The two urban centers, Seattle and Tacoma, have student populations of about 45,000 and 30,000, respectively, or approximately 25% of the total student group. While Tacoma's student group size is about the same as it was during the 1960s, Seattle's has been cut in half.

The university, which was launched with but one professor in 1861, today houses about 34,000 students and a teaching and research faculty of 3,160. Its 128 buildings are spread over 694 acres in north-central Seattle. The largest university in the state, its reputation as a leading center for learning and research is well established.

The College of Education, when fully staffed, has a faculty of 65, which, as a result of retrenchment, is down from 90 over the past decade. The college enrollment is limited by the university's provost to a maximum of 504 graduate-degree students and 250 licensure students, which makes it a relatively small unit. However, because the college views its role as one of creating knowledge more than of providing direct training to large numbers of education students, this is not a major problem. As the current dean notes, his and the faculty's job is to "keep the pot boiling, to be on thin ice, figuring out how to do it better, to change the givens, see if it works, and then decide what to do with it."

Because of the enrollment limits set by the provost, as well as the existence of several other universities in the area (Seattle University, Seattle Pacific University, the University of Puget Sound, and a branch of Western Washington), the college is indeed in a distinctively advantageous position to pursue cutting-edge directions.

Educational Leadership and Policy Studies is one of four areas in the College of Education. The others are Curriculum and Instruction, Educational Psychology, and Special Education.

The Leadership and Policy Studies Area houses 11 tenure-track faculty lines (2 of which are not filled) and several others on research appointments. Formed in the early 1980s, it includes educational administration, higher education, and social foundations. In the decade that the area has been in existence, these traditional disciplines have been brought into a closely knit academic community, a community that provides necessary research and teaching support to its members' programs. Those faculty who are most concerned with general policy issues, about half of the area's faculty group, are most closely associated with the preparation of educational leaders.

The area serves 201 graduate students, 104 of whom are seeking one of Washington state's three administrator certificates: 65 for principal licenses, 14 for program administrators, 9 for both of these certificates, and 16 for the superintendent certificate. About one third of those seeking principal certificates are also enrolled in M.Ed. programs. Of the area's 86 doctoral students, 37 are in higher education, and the rest are concentrating on educational leadership and policy studies.

Readiness for Change

The Educational Leadership and Policy Studies Area had already started to rethink its preparation program by the mid-1980s. It was even conducting a study for the Office of the State Superintendent of Public Instruction concerning administrator preparation when it was challenged to rethink its preparation program and join the Danforth Foundation's second cycle of university programs.

To their credit, the faculty was not complacent about the status-quo program, even though it had won a prestigious award. In fact, even prior to the Danforth challenge, faculty members, sensitive to the demands for change emanating from the educational-reform movement, were discussing the need to instill more emphasis on the clinical component of the program. Given the openness to new ideas, as well as the fact that several faculty positions were soon going to be filled, new appointments, if carefully made, could support the area's ability to change. The timing for such a review was fortuitous.

Initially, several faculty members, including the area chairperson (who has since left to become the dean of a college of education), another faculty member who later replaced him as chairperson, a doctoral student working as a research assistant (who had just completed 15 years as a teacher and administrator, and who later became the coordinator of the program), and an elementary principal, met to explore program ideas.

The central role played by the field administrator, who has remained a key partner in the effort, set a positive tone for further partner relationships. The group quickly agreed that in order to create a relevant program and to promote meaningful partnerships between the area and the school community, the planning group should be expanded to include field-based leaders throughout the region.

Fortunately, the college had worked with area school leaders to create, in 1985, the Puget Sound Educational Consortium, which included many of the leading school districts in the area. The consortium evolved out of several years of informal interactions around ideas and issues. Once formed, it created an opportunity for the region's educational leaders to form a positive partnership to improve delivery of educational services. The consortium is sufficiently valued by its member school districts that they proportionately share in supporting its annual budget of more than $250,000.

The purposes of the consortium, the administrative unit of which is housed in the College of Education, are to promote cooperative endeavors between the College of Education and the educational community, to stimulate growth and development, and to explore educational policy issues confronting member school districts. The consortium sponsors many activities in support of its purposes, including conferences, academies, task forces, and demonstration centers.

The small planning group mentioned earlier, composed of the chairperson, the doctoral student, and the faculty member who later became the next chairperson, brought skeletal ideas to the consortium, which then included 10 school districts, represented by superintendents and deputy superintendents. There was enthusiastic support for the ideas and a desire to become active partners in the project.

Participation was initially limited to candidates sponsored by districts represented in the consortium, but this restriction has been dropped, and participants now come from school districts throughout the region. The program was opened to other candidates in 1990 because the chairperson was concerned about the issue of open access to a public institution.

The partnership was made operational in two ways. First, eight member districts made initial commitments to sponsor full-time releases (later scaled back to half-time releases as a minimum commitment), for one or more of their teachers. Equally important, consortium members agreed to join the area faculty in planning for and monitoring the progress of the proposed program by establishing a Program Design Committee. The committee comprises one administrator; either a central office leader or a principal, representing each of the participating school districts; and faculty members from the area, several of whom are not in the small planning group. As is noted later, the partnering concept has been further extended by the establishment of other committees for specific curricular purposes.

The Program Design Committee quickly agreed that the established program was deficient in several ways:

1. It was constrained to the traditional three-credit course approach.
2. There was no sequential set of learning experiences.
3. It did not have a rigorously supervised clinical component.
4. Admissions were based on academic criteria only.
5. Students were self-selected.

The committee concluded that it wanted to make preparation more directly relevant to leadership development. Specific objectives focused on the following:

1. Developing strong partnerships with school leaders in the region and including these partners in the dialogue and decision making about overall values and program intent
2. Delivering meaningful content and doing so when content-related issues (e.g., budget) would be a high-priority topic in school settings

3. Moving away from the 3-hour course approach and replacing it with flexible and variable-length educational units

4. Establishing thematic approaches to guide the election and development of content

5. Significantly increasing the proportion of the program devoted to field experiences and making those experiences more rigorous

6. Focused recruiting, with the intention of increasing ethnic and racial minority participation in the program, given the increasing and shifting minority population in the Puget Sound area

In short, the Program Design Committee decided to challenge the givens that had guided the area's program efforts until that time. The reference point became relevance rather than format. Everything was to be tested against this reference point and, if found wanting, was to be modified or even discarded as experience accumulated. This attitude—everything is open to review by all partners—remains a cornerstone and a primary strength of the program.

By June of 1988, values and purpose were agreed on. However, the detailed curriculum and instructional design still needed to be developed. During June and July of that year, a small planning group created the design, and the program began that August.

The fact that the area has replaced its traditional program with the Danforth experimental program is evidence that the effort has been successful. As the dean noted, "Good innovations should be institutionalized, and when that happens, you can't continue to justify the existing program."

DESCRIPTION OF THE PROGRAM

To guide development of the program, the Program Design Committee debated and agreed on a set of "working assumptions," which have evolved over time to include the following:

Equity and Excellence—High-quality education for all students is a viable and morally correct goal.

Leadership—Management skills constitute an important component, but leaders also need to articulate, justify, and protect core values that constitute the purposes and functions
of schools.

Organizational Change—Schools need to be self-renewing. The
leader's role is to help initiate, implement, and evaluate that
process.

Collaboration—Leaders must facilitate widespread involvement
in the renewal of schools.

Inquiry and Reflective Practice—Leaders must value and have the
ability to reflect critically about their schools' dynamics and
to promote this value and skill in others.

These working assumptions, which the area faculty supports,
provide the foundation for program development. They are disseminated widely—for example, in recruitment literature and program
descriptions—but not just for public relations purposes. They continue to serve as the basis for decision making about program relevance and change.

State certification requirements (the Washington Administrative
Code) are considered, but only to be certain that state expectations are
encompassed. They are not driving forces for the program. Certification requirements for principals and program administrators include
a minimum of 180 days of teaching experience, a bachelor's degree,
and a preparation program approved by the Office of the Superintendent of Public Instruction. Also included are knowledge and skills in
specific areas (e.g., the development and organization of education,
student activities, auxiliary services, and school law), and an internship of at least 320 hours. Compliance is verified by site mentors
signing a form indicating that interns have been engaged with these
activities. The area chairperson then signs off and submits supportive
data to the Certification Office in the Office of the State Superintendent of Public Instruction.

Curriculum design committees, composed of interested faculty
members, school leaders, alumni and current students, meet to establish the purposes, overall content, instructional design, and sequencing of academic units. In the first 2 years, these committees met
regularly, as the program was being specified and detailed. Currently,

they meet when evaluative feedback indicates the need to modify instructional units or to add new ones. The coordinator is responsible for monitoring the system and calling the committees together when appropriate.

ACADEMIC CONTENT AND DELIVERY

Required Coursework

Students who already have a master's degree (most Washington school districts require a master's degree for administrative positions) take 36 quarter hours over a period of 11 months (five quarters). The sequence begins in August, with registration in the second summer quarter; continues through the academic year with the fall, winter, and spring quarters; and concludes with the first summer session the following June. Those who do not possess an M.Ed. degree must take a minimum of another 12 quarter hours to complete the degree. Typically, about one third of the student group requires the M.Ed. degree.

Delivery of Instruction

Instruction is delivered in ways that fit the needs of the learner and the realities of the workplace, rather than according to traditional academic expectations. In this regard, courses per se do not exist. Rather, major "themes" (described later) are pursued, with specific content delivered according to when it is a focal point of interest in schools. For example, among other times, issues related to finance and budget are explored when site-based decisions about school budgets are being made during the early spring months.

This approach requires extensive planning and a willingness to deliver academic content as it fits students' learning needs, rather than when it is convenient for the instructors. It also requires that the coordinator stay in contact with school leaders and the cohort to get feedback, share this information with instructors, and negotiate adjustments to the schedule of presentations to ensure that the curriculum is delivered when and as needed.

It requires creativity and ingenuity to maintain such a flexible approach to the delivery of the curriculum. The program is embedded in a university, a complex organization that tends to insist on uniformity and regularity in the structuring of academic experiences. Initially, the planners got around this issue simply by registering cohort members as though they were taking standard area courses (finance, law, personnel, program administration, organizational theory, and planning and evaluation), but delivering instruction as needed.

A more manageable system has now been developed. Beginning with the 1992 academic year, the program will go to a 5-quarter approach, with a specific title given to each quarter, variable credit hours (3 to 6, with a maximum of 9) in the course catalog, with the specific number of hours actually assigned based on the content and the effort required.

This unique approach emanated from the planners' belief that a good program must emphasize quality, and that everything must be done to ensure that quality. In pursuit of this end, the planners decided not to become overly concerned about university expectations such as maintaining high numbers of student credit hours.

Sequence of Activities

The first quarter, which takes place in August of the first summer, is devoted to three activities: a 10-day residential experience, 5 days at the first internship site, and, finally, 5 days devoted to academic content.

Activity 1. The residential experience, which takes place on the University of Washington campus, is also the first time that the group comes together. The focus is on cohort development—that is, the creation of a community of learners who will support and challenge each other to take risks to grow and become effective educational leaders. Students, who live together in dormitory suites, pay tuition (which is $110 per credit in the summer, and $162 per credit during the academic year), $100 for materials, and $350 for room and board. With the exception of a midweek half-day break, participants take part in highly structured experiences from 8:30 in the morning through 9:00 in the evening.

The instructional team is composed of area faculty members, the coordinator, and practitioners with extensive backgrounds in organization development who use role playing, simulations, case studies, and other interactive techniques to encourage self-awareness, confidence building, and team development. The team also emphasizes facilitation skills needed by educational leaders, including goal setting, communications, decision making, problem solving, and conflict management.

As one of the instructors referred to this intensive program kick-off, it is an attempt to get students "from head to heart, from past to future" in their approach and thinking. At the request of the cohort, these instructors may come back for further sessions during the academic year.

Three other activities take place during this 10-day session. First, based on a set of readings that is sent to students early in the summer, seminars are held to introduce them to some basic concepts about leadership and about issues confronting the schools. The idea is to establish a common framework of reference and also to set the norm that reading, discourse, and critical thinking are important and are an expectation of the program.

Next, the major themes of the year's curriculum are introduced. Instructors who will be working with students on instructional units related to these themes during the coming academic year spend evenings introducing purposes and content. Finally, students receive basic information about potential internship sites and are encouraged to sort this information and make initial contacts with site supervisors (called mentors).

Activity 2. This involves another 5-day, but nonresidential, session on campus, devoted to a unit on educational law and an introduction to portraiture, which is described in a later section.

Activity 3. This involves a 5-day introduction to the first internship site. Interns work with mentors in preparation for the opening of school.

Course Design and Content

During the regular academic year, the cohort gathers for formal instructional purposes every Thursday afternoon for 6 hours and approximately one Saturday every month for 7 hours. Initially, the group met for 3 hours on Tuesday and 3 hours on Friday, rather than for 6 hours on Thursday. The modified design was implemented because students and districts were critical about the extra travel and the amount of time away from school sites that were required. The faculty's understanding and responsiveness to this concern was symbolically important; that is, it provided early evidence that the area really intended to follow through on feedback that was offered to increase relevance and effectiveness. The use of Saturdays built on the area's long-established use of this weekend day for program purposes. Maintaining use of this lengthy period of time is viewed as vital to ensuring adequate coverage and time to discuss issues and experiences.

Using daytime hours on Thursdays weekly and on Saturdays monthly to bring the cohort together for instructional purposes also has a positive effect on learning. Rather than coming together at the end of a long work day, as is the case in most programs, participants arrive with enthusiasm and energy.

A typical Thursday session includes several segments. About 1½ hours are devoted to a reflective seminar, during which the coordinator and the cohort examine dynamics that have been occurring in internship experiences (what is working, what is not working, and why). They discuss those issues identified at the outset of the program, as well as those identified as the year progresses. Students often research these issues and share the resultant information. Opportunity is provided for personal feedback from peers. By November, students are invited to voluntarily facilitate some of these sessions.

The rest of the afternoon is usually devoted to one or more academic units. Curriculum planning begins with the assumption that content should be delivered when and how it is appropriate, rather than in the three-credit, 3-hour blocks that typify traditional programs. Units vary in scope, as well as in time given for delivery of instruction, depending on the Program Design Committee's estimation of need and relevance, which is measured against the program's basic assumptions. Although some units resemble traditional topical areas such as supervision, curriculum, finance, and evaluation, others cover more novel content areas, such as moral leadership, portraiture, student and faculty diversity, and student-generated learning.

Academic sessions are typically highly interactive. For example, one Thursday session focused on two brief units—lessons from the Foxfire experiments, and the principal's role in site-based budgeting. Both involved exercises, small-group work, and large-group dialogue, and both focused on meaning for school leadership.

There are two overarching program themes that continue throughout the year and that provide guidance and coherence to the program, as well as a solid basis from which to develop instructional units. The first theme, *Inquiry, Organizations, and Educational Change,* seeks to change students' mind maps from those of teachers to those of administrators, and from classroom to school and school system. This theme, which cuts across the working assumptions of the program, is recognized as a critical element for effective leadership. Students are introduced to methodological tools for the critical analysis of schools and organizational change. The questions posed delve below the surface level and encourage students to think about the complex and important underpinnings of values-driven decision making, which crosses over into the second theme.

The second theme, *Moral Dimensions of Leadership,* encourages students to view schools as moral institutions and provides the skills to determine the culture of the schools they will lead. Students learn the language and definitions regarding moral organizations, focus on interpersonal moral dilemmas, and analyze moral dilemmas for schools (e.g., What are the effects of compulsory education on schools and for their own school sites specifically?). As with the change theme, the moral dimensions theme cuts across the working assumptions on which the program is based. This theme, which is not found in most preparation programs, is clearly important because resource decisions concerning time, human inputs, materials, and funds are value driven.

A major element that runs throughout the program focuses on *multiculturalism.* Given the basic program assumption concerning equity and excellence, the academic content includes an emphasis on multicultural issues. The major issue has to do with sensitizing cohort members, many of whom come from suburban environments, to the need to ensure that all learners have the best possible chance to succeed, regardless of racial, ethnic, or other diversity realities. The value base is to be inclusive, rather than exclusive. As with the major themes, multiculturalistic content includes exploring questions and concerns, providing an overview and definitions, examining trends and problems, connecting school effectiveness to equity concepts, and developing skills to effect needed changes. Activities for each student include site assessments, problem identification, exercises, strategies to reconfigure curriculums as appropriate, and action planning. As the instructor noted, it is an attempt to get past the "tacos on Tuesday" approach to a more comprehensive multiculturalism approach.

The multiculturalism unit is not the only way students encounter this concept. The diverse composition of the cohort group and the differences in their field site situations inevitably lead to continuing discussions about multicultural issues in academic presentations, reflective seminars, and informal interactions. A newly created Center for Multicultural Education in the College will become a useful resource to maintain and expand the program's focus on this area.

Synthesis

The final academic experience, which takes place during the last week in June, is a 5-day synthesizing experience. The session is cooperatively planned with students who volunteer for this activity and who also develop and facilitate simulations to meet program intent. Because the cohort group helps set the agenda for the 5 days, specific content may vary (e.g., opening a school or restructuring) but the goal remains the same: personal reflection, making the transition into the profession of administration, and program evaluation and redesign. Students are introduced to this week of introspection through the many shorter opportunities they have to reflect during the academic year: reflective seminars, self-analysis exercises, and regular feedback about academic performance. The coordinator also offers four seminars, each 2 to 3 hours in length, focusing on activities associated with obtaining a position (mock interviews, placement services, writing résumés, and setting up files), which students may choose to take all or part of on a voluntary, noncredit basis.

Assumptions About Learning

Three learning assumptions permeate the academic curriculum. The first focuses on the need to become reflective, to have increased sensitivity to and skill in understanding self and environment. The more that cohort members understand themselves, the more clearly they will understand and identify with their core beliefs, leadership styles, and decision-making biases. Activities include intensive introspective exercises (including development of "life maps") during the 10-day residential experience, journal writing, discussions in reflective seminars, writing "curriculum autobiographies" (i.e., how students come to the beliefs they hold about education), purposeful probing—both one-on-one and in groups led by the program coordinator, and dialogues with site mentors.

The second assumption focuses on the need for community building and the importance of collaborative working groups, both of which require understanding of the schools' organizational dynamics. A variety of activities centering on cohort development (e.g., the 10-day summer institute, students sharing all academic experiences, shared site visits, and formal and informal social gatherings) provide opportunities to do community building. Students come to value the support they gain from associating with each other, as well as the networking opportunities they create for the rest of their careers. Equally important, as several program alumni noted, they are sensitized to the need to transfer this immediate sense of community to the organizations they will soon lead. The more they know about their organizational and community environments, the more effective they will be as leaders of adult and learner communities.

The second assumption is also facilitated by a unique program element called *portraiture*, which is a method of identifying and specifying organizational cultures through ethnographic observations. During the first summer quarter, students receive brief organizational portraits that have been developed for review and selection of internship sites. During the fall, they receive up to 24 hours of instruction in the purpose of portraiture and in the skills needed to create these portraits (interviewing, observing, keeping field notes, determining patterns), and they then develop a portrait of their internship sites.

The third assumption, which has to do with the purposeful integration of academic content and clinical experiences, occurs in several ways. Already noted is the effort the Program Design Committee gives to introducing academic content according to when it is likely to be encountered in the flow of events at schools. Further, instructors are encouraged to bring seminar content to life by creating assignments that require site activities such as observations, interviews, surveys, and diagnostic exercises; making site visits with students that center around relevant issues (e.g., the coordinator, who teaches the unit on Planning and Evaluation, includes three to five visits of 6 hours each at sites that are engaging in related activities); and asking educational leaders who are dealing with issues being covered to make presentations and lead discussions at seminars. Further, the curriculum is modified at least annually to incorporate issues that are of concern to educational leaders. For example, last year, business partnerships and social service connections were included. This year, site-based management and restructuring have become central topics for the cohort group.

Faculty

Instruction is delivered by educational leaders from surrounding school districts, as well as by full-time faculty. In fact, typically, about 50% of the content is delivered by field leaders who are granted adjunct faculty status. Besides coming in to do single sessions on a voluntary basis and hosting the cohort, when requested, at their educational sites, these adjuncts are paid to teach specific units. During the current academic year, 7 of the 13 instructors in the program are school-district leaders. For example, the law unit is being taught by a school-district legal counsel, the multicultural unit is being taught by a director of curriculum and instruction, one of the 10-day residential session instructors is a local elementary school principal, supervision of instruction is taught by an assistant superintendent for instruction, and the portraiture instructor is a school-district superintendent.

The intention to use adjuncts in this manner was established at the outset. The quality of instruction was the guiding factor. As the current chairperson noted, "We want instruction delivered by experts. When practitioners are more expert than us, we will pay them to do it." When the requisite curriculum was identified, it soon became clear that it could not all be delivered by current faculty, both for lack of expertise and because of their many additional responsibilities. Further, the enrichment offered leading practitioners, carefully selected for their knowledge and their instructional reputations, expands the area's ability to remain flexible as it responds to shifting leadership preparation needs.

Practitioners play another important instructional role. Because of the recognition that academic content becomes meaningful to students if they see how it applies to site-based leadership activities, the faculty attempts to include mentors in the instructional loop. This is done by updating them regularly regarding the focus of the Thursday and Saturday seminars. They are encouraged to have discussions with their interns about academic learnings and to provide them with on-site opportunities to extend these learnings.

Evaluation

Evaluation is a deeply embedded value. A number of evaluation activities encourage students and faculty to become more reflective and to seek individual and programmatic improvements. Evaluation is also conducted as a form of role modeling, in the hope that students will value this important activity in their leadership efforts. Students are evaluated in a variety of ways, including formal and informal feedback from site mentors; unit instructors' responses to written assignments and group participation exercises; the coordinator's feedback about their progress and growth; and, perhaps most important, opportunities for introspection and for receiving feedback from cohort members.

Faculty receive considerably more evaluative feedback than they would in traditional programs. Specifically, after the completion of a unit, the coordinator meets with the cohort and elicits responses to the content and the instructor. She then meets privately with the instructor and shares the group's overall assessment. The purpose is to encourage continued behaviors when appropriate and to suggest changes if needed.

The program is evaluated quarterly. Full-time faculty and adjunct faculty who are teaching in the program during that academic year come together as an instructional team to explore the effectiveness of the curriculum. The coordinator, who systematically collects evaluative data for individual units, as well as for the overall program, acts as the facilitator, encouraging the group to reflect about the program and to make adjustments as required, even while the program is in progress. The agenda she prepares typically includes opportunities to revisit the program's working assumptions, syntheses of evaluative data, and key questions to guide the discussion. The group looks at redundancies and omissions, with the intention of updating the curriculum of the program. As an example of the value of these meetings, recent evaluative data indicated that students felt uncomfortable about supervising staff members who are perceived to be poor teachers. As a result of this feedback, the instructional team recommended that a new unit on teaching and learning be added to the curriculum. This unit was introduced by the Planning Design Committee this year.

It is important to note that practitioners are included in these instructional team sessions. This ensures that practitioner concerns and needs are regularly considered and that the program is more likely to remain relevant. It also models and supports the value of collaborative partnership. As one district leader noted, "We decide with the university—that's power!"

Interestingly, one traditional evaluation device, formal grading, is downplayed in the program. Those seeking only certification are not graded, receiving only credit/no credit on their transcripts. Those seeking an M.Ed. must be graded in accord with university rules, but even they are not graded on their clinical experiences. Resistance to formal grading does not imply unwillingness to evaluate, but rather a hesitance to employ an evaluation approach that is rarely helpful for students' growth and development.

STUDENTS

Initially, the program was available exclusively to candidates sponsored by participating school districts from the Puget Sound Educational Consortium. This restriction has been removed, partly because participating districts have only been able to finance internships for one or two interns, so the potential pool of candidates was not large enough and also partly because the faculty felt that it was their obligation to serve the entire educational community rather than a few select school districts. Further, although most candidates continue to be nominated and sponsored by school districts, the faculty has made a few exceptions. For example, three current interns are from out of state. One is providing his own financial support so that he can meet internship requirements, another has sabbatical leave support from her district, and a third is a teaching assistant in the Curriculum and Instruction Area.

Cohort members have come from between 10 and 14 school districts. Maximum cohort size was initially set at 15, but the number of students admitted totaled only 14 the first year, 13 the second year, and 12 the third year. The maximum cohort size was increased to 20, starting with the fourth year, mainly because the decision to institutionalize the program has created a concern about student credit hours. This need, as well as the concern for creating a fair opportunity for all school districts to participate, led to the decision to allow other districts' candidates to apply, and to a more vigorous and purposeful recruiting effort. The potential pool has increased significantly, and the cohort size has shown parallel growth. This year's group is 20, and it is expected that the group that will start this summer, which was selected out of an applicant pool of 35, will also be 20.

For the first 4 years, the demographic breakdown includes 37% males and 63% females, which is a better male intake level than is the case in many preparation programs today. The racial and ethnic majority/minority mix is 71% European-American, 17% African-American, 7% Asian-American, and 5% Hispanic-American. The minority percentage is fairly representative of the region's school professional population and is much better than the area and the college have typically attracted.

School districts make initial nominations. Each uses its own process, but all are guided by several factors. First, candidates must have a minimum of 3 years of experience as teachers or in related roles, such as counselor or reading specialist. Second, the focus is on candidates' potential as leaders, as measured by experience in leadership positions, indicators of high commitment, demonstrated positive communications and human relations skills, strong peer ratings, and evidence of ability to understand and respond to educational issues. The availability of the program is advertised throughout the district; interested individuals develop application files, which typically include letters of recommendation from their principals, statements of purpose/goals, and evidence of academic ability. A review committee examines the files to ensure that criteria are met, and it invites qualified candidates to an interview session. Names of those approved by the committee are sent to the area.

Candidates fill out a standard admissions application, with one notable exception—recommendations, which are made on a form focusing on leadership potential, must come from the candidate's principal, a teacher of the principal's choice, and a second teacher identified by the candidate. Candidates are then invited to take part in an interview that explores their values and the degree of clarity they have about how they would act on those values in leadership roles, and a 1-hour essay exercise that focuses on how they would lead, given the changing demographics and dynamics challenging today's schools. The results of the interview and essay are collaboratively rated by a review team formed by the coordinator, which includes area faculty members, practitioners, alumni, and current interns. The coordinator and other key faculty participants check outcomes to be sure that all required information is included. The faculty reserves final judgment for itself, honoring the long-held tradition that graduate-school admissions is a faculty prerogative and responsibility.

The quality of the student cohort is perceived to be good, but there have been no hard data collected to substantiate this perception. Faculty members frequently comment about cohort members' intensity, focus, and commitment to high performance. Similar comments are made by adjunct instructors. For example, the adjunct who teaches law also teaches a traditional law course for another university. Although she does not feel that, as a group, the cohort members are brighter, she is certain that they are more energized and interactive. This makes her teaching efforts more complicated, but also more fun.

Program graduates are able to find administrative positions. As of May 1992, of the 39 current graduates, 15 were in principalships, 5 were in assistant/associate principalships, 8 were in central-office director positions, and 11 were still in the classroom. This high placement record (72%) is probably due to a combination of factors, including the fact that students are sponsored by their districts, which have invested heavily in their preparation and thus have a stake in their career growth; the quality and intensity of the preparation program; and the visibility that graduates gain through their several internship experiences.

In contrast, data concerning graduates of the traditional program for the 1989-1990 and 1990-1991 academic years show placement of 25%, or 17 of 67 students who took the program at that time. This low figure is partially explained by the fact that many did not choose to search for positions, some did not complete their studies, and a few went directly into a doctoral program. However, even with these factors taken into consideration, the difference is noticeable.

The area attempts to maintain contact with graduates through several means. Informal communications are pursued by the coordinator when graduates seek advice in finding positions, as well as when they encounter leadership dilemmas once in these positions. She sends follow-up surveys at regular intervals to get continuing input about the program, as well as about graduates' career status. Alumni are invited to participate on different committees (e.g., planning, curriculum, and admissions), and a series of four follow-up seminars is organized each year for program graduates, centering on current topical areas of interest (about 45 attend one or more sessions each year, at a cost of $20 per student for the series). These activities serve to promote continuing professional development for graduates and to encourage the development of an ever-widening network of educators committed to the continuation of program purposes.

INTERNSHIP

Time-on-task in clinical settings is extensive. Originally, the intent was to require a full-time internship for all cohort members. It soon became clear that this could not be achieved in all participating school districts because of budgetary limitations. Therefore, it was agreed that a minimum requirement would be for half-time internships. This translates to a minimum of 12 hours per week (4 days × 3 hours) because interns are at their sites 4 days a week, with the fifth day, Thursday, being reserved for on-campus reflective seminars and educational units.

In reality, few districts provide sufficient resources so that their candidates are able to focus full-time on their internships. In this year's cohort, about half of the group have full-time internships. The time-on-task that cohort members receive in their clinical settings is extensive, approximately 1400 hours for full-time interns and 700 hours for half-time interns. Even for those with half-time internships, the time-on-task is still above the average (632 hours) for all participating Danforth institutions.

All but a few cohort members are granted release time by school districts for internship activities. However, to promote access to the program, the area does encourage alternatives to district sponsorship. Options include using a sabbatical year, taking personal leave, seeking university financial support (scholarships and fellowships), and having districts create quasi-administrative positions that can be used to serve as a means of creating internship opportunities. Thus far, 7 of the 59 participants in the program have used alternative strategies to district provision of release time.

The extensive time available for the internship provides a solid base for learning, while the structural elements guiding that effort enhance the potential for high-quality leadership preparation. These elements include the following: highly selective internship sites, orientation sessions, internship experiences, hands-on experiences, weekly reflective seminars, faculty supervision of fieldwork, and site mentors.

Highly Selective Choices of Internship Sites. The pool of sites and site supervisors is formed on the basis of careful screening. Each district has a high-level administrator serving on the Program Design Committee who is asked to make initial recommendations of potential mentors. If interested, the mentor nominee is asked to secure several peer recommendations and to create a portfolio, or set of "exhibits," which describes the school, its program, staff, and community situation. Following this, a team (typically, someone from the Program Design Committee and one or two others of their choice, often including a program graduate or a current intern) visits the site for a day, to develop a report, or miniportrait, that describes site dynamics and the leadership behavior of the principal. The Program Design Committee reviews the report and the exhibits and makes final decisions.

Selected administrators sign a "Mentor-Principal Letter of Commitment," which includes a detailed description of the nature of their role and the extent of their involvement. A pool of about 30 mentors/sites is maintained and updated through this process.

Because flexibility is intentionally included as an attribute of the program, cohort members are also permitted to suggest alternative sites/mentors. If the Program Design Committee thinks that such alternatives would provide positive learning situations, interns are permitted to include one such experience during the year. If the experience is positive, it is likely that the principal will be nominated as a mentor. A team will then create a portrait so that the site may be considered for addition to the pool.

Orientation Session. During the 10-day residential session, cohort members are introduced to the purposes of the internship and are given opportunities to review site portraits and a set of exhibits collected by the site principal that describe the school (e.g., programs, staff, community) through text, pictures, and even videos. Students set up interviews with mentors with whom they would like to work for the first quarter (the coordinator makes sure that only one intern visits a particular site). If the interview is positive, the mentoring relationship is established. If it is not, the process is repeated. Besides increasing the likelihood of a positive internship experience, the process also provides an early opportunity to learn how one goes about the process of obtaining a leadership position.

Internship Experiences. Cohort members are required to have three different internship experiences, spread across three academic quarters from September through June. The intent is to help them broaden perspectives, observe different leadership styles, and enhance sensitivity to diversity. Normally, students are expected to have at least two of their three internship experiences outside of their own school district, at least one at a level that is different from the one at which they intend to become an administrator, and at least one in a demographically different setting (usually, this means an urban experience). Interns pursue the aforementioned process for each of these experiences.

The fact that interns serve in three different sites multiplies the potential for learning. Different levels, types of communities, and leadership styles of their mentors are all elements that positively influence this rich learning situation.

Hands-On Experiences. The focus is on hands-on experiences rather than shadowing and observing. Interns develop an "Internship Plan," which is reviewed by the university supervisor and the site mentor. These plans, which include purposes, activities, and evaluation approaches, are completed and agreed on at the outset of the quarter, so that the intern can quickly take on responsibility for a set of administrative activities. For example, one intern is doing research on alternative assessment approaches at her school site, meeting with teachers and parents regarding multiage grouping issues, writing a staff handbook, and working with the principal to supervise and evaluate teaching in the school.

Weekly Reflective Seminars. Weekly reflective seminars provide continuing opportunities to diagnose and analyze site dynamics. They also provide opportunities for the coordinator to get an update on the realities of these situations and to know whether she needs to intervene in any of them.

Faculty Supervision of Fieldwork. Full-time tenure-track faculty members, as well as the coordinator, are assigned to field-supervision activities. This enhances the potential that seminar presentations of faculty members who teach educational units will be reality based and that students' overall learning experiences will be integrated. Indicative of the importance placed on this activity, faculty members are given a course reduction in their teaching loads of two courses per quarter for every four students they supervise. The load reduction is a recognition of the effort required and a means of allowing faculty to maintain their focus on research and publication.

Site Mentors. Site mentors, who are carefully selected, participate in mentor sessions that increase the likelihood of meaningful internship experiences. Initially, they attend a half-day orientation session, during which they are introduced to mentor role expectations. Subsequently, they meet as a group once each quarter to share concerns and ideas about their experience and to be updated by the coordinator regarding the current emphasis of the academic program and ways that they might be able to enhance interns' learnings by pursuing parallel site-based activities. In addition, the field supervisor meets at least twice per quarter with the intern and mentor, early on, to clarify expectations and later to review outcomes and learnings.

Site mentors, in most instances, receive no compensation for their efforts. The only extrinsic reward is library privileges at the university, the aforementioned quarterly work sessions, which include a sponsored dinner, and an open invitation to attend the Thursday and Saturday class sessions. They are also invited to follow-up seminars, along with program graduates (on average, mentors represent about 50% of the participants in these sessions).

COORDINATION

Coordination was minimal during the first program year, which led to much confusion. Since the second year, the program has been guided by a full-time coordinator. She is unique among Danforth program coordinators, in that throughout the experience, she has been a doctoral student in the area. Her extensive school-level and district-level administrative experience, knowledge of the region, demonstrated scholarship, and strong interpersonal skills have more than overcome potential problems. In fact, all parties agree that her understanding of and good-natured irreverence for the rules and constraints of both settings—school systems and the university—enable her to function very effectively on behalf of the cohort.

There is also substantial faculty and management support of the coordinator. The first chairperson, who left the university 1 year into the program, initially shared in the development of the program concept with the current coordinator. The current chairperson was carefully socialized by the earlier chairperson about his key role in the Danforth program and, as an individual, demonstrates a strong belief in the purposes and processes of the program. Three other faculty members provide supervision for interns. One of them has been responsible for the bulk of field supervision and values this activity not only for what it does for interns, but also for how it informs him of practice, stimulates his ideas, and provides data for his research. Other area and college faculty members teach units in the program when requested to do so.

FINANCIAL ARRANGEMENTS

Relative to other Danforth programs, the area has found itself in a good financial situation. The districts' continuing commitment to full- and half-time releases for internships has been maintained despite an overall recessionary climate in the state. Washington schools are heavily funded from the state level, so even though Puget Sound's economy is stronger than the rest of the state, school districts are in a precarious budgetary position.

In addition, nondegree (certification only) students pay tuition through continuing education. Many of these dollars have been returned to the area for use in a variety of ways, including support for the coordinator's salary and pay for adjunct instructors. This practice will end now that the Danforth program is becoming the area's only preparation program. Now it becomes more important to be able to count student contact hours. Payment will be processed through the bursar's office, and the area will no longer have access to these funds.

Students make direct funding contributions in several ways. As noted, they pay for room and board for the summer residential experience, for educational materials each quarter, and, in most cases, for their own tuition. Currently, one quarter of the coordinator's salary is supported by the College of Education. This amount will be fully funded by the college as of the current fiscal year, despite the fact that the college will not receive any additional allocations from the university and may actually have to cope with a small reduction in its budget. This is a strong indication of the support and the high priority being given to the program by the college. As the dean noted, if it is important, "You've got to suck it up . . . if it is right we have to pay for it." The area also seeks other funds, beyond those provided by the Danforth Foundation, to support program needs. For example, 1 year, it received a grant from the Office of the State Superintendent of Public Instruction to support an assessment center, which was used as an exiting experience at the end of the program. Money is also available from the Corbally Fund, an endowment for innovative developments, instructional uses, and networking activities in the college administrative programs. Follow-up seminars for graduates include a $20 charge, which provides a small but flexible budgetary support for program-related activities.

In short, all parties play a role in financing the program. Students pay for the summer residential program, materials, and tuition. Districts pay for release time to complete internships. The university pays some of the coordinator's salary and provides part of faculty members' load time for supervisory and instructional activities.

Analysis

Having completed almost four cycles of cohort groups, the University of Washington has come a long way toward the development of a coherent and relevant approach to leadership preparation. What is particularly impressive is that even after 4 years, major program changes, and heavy expenditure of energy, there is still a sense of excitement and of involvement in the creation of something important. This excitement is noticeable on the part of students, mentors, key district officials, adjunct instructors, the coordinator, the chairperson, and some of the faculty. In fact, almost everyone appears to be enthusiastic about phasing out the traditional program and institutionalizing the experimental program. Clearly, there are payoffs for all participants.

Payoffs for Students

For graduates, the most obvious payoff is the attainment of a high-priority goal—that is, becoming an administrator, which has occurred for about three out of four graduates, as compared to about one out of four of those going through the traditional program. Beyond this, however, there are a number of other recognized important positive outcomes, two of which are relatively unique to this program.

First, the careful attention given to balancing and integrating the academic program with the clinical experience increases the likelihood of well-rounded graduates who can appreciate and comprehend important concepts and information while also being able to reflect on practice and to provide outstanding leadership for schools. One faculty member who stays in contact with graduates noted that they continue to seek out readings, reflect on practice, and worry about issues such as equity. In support of this perception, a school walk-through with a graduate of the first cohort who is a principal in a site-based management situation indicated that she is able to analyze complex organizational dynamics and take action, when appropriate, to improve the situation. Similarly, the adjunct instructor responsible for the multicultural unit reports that graduates call on her to seek advice in implementing diversity programs in their schools.

Second, the focus on moral decision making changes students' thinking, getting them more in touch with their basic values, as well as those of the organizations in which they work. As one graduate noted, "I look at more points of view now." In fact, this graduate is a member of an ethnic minority and will soon move from a middle-class community teaching position to become a principal in a core area urban school. She has chosen to do so because the requirement of exploring moral values has convinced her that she should do this, both for herself and for the contributions she now believes she needs to make to help racial and ethnic minorities progress in our society.

For current students, the perceptions of benefits have more to do with the present year (although, as of the end of May 1992, five cohort members have already been hired—three as principals and two as assistant principals, which is an impetus that will probably turn the focus of interest of others toward this long-term goal). Generally, the feeling is that the program is among the best learning experiences these adult learners have encountered for the following reasons:

1. It includes them as partners in establishing a relevant curriculum.

2. It is delivered in a highly interactive manner by experts coming from the field, as well as from the university.

3. It promotes transformational thinking, due to inclusion of content such as moral leadership and organizational change, as well as introspective exercises such as life maps, reflective journals, and portraits.

4. The emphasis on cohorts provides training in collaborative leadership as well as support and networking opportunities.

5. It exposes them to high-quality mentors who can help them clarify their administrative belief systems and their leadership styles.

6. It integrates field experiences with on-campus learnings, particularly through weekly reflective seminars. There is an upbeat attitude, even as the work load intensifies. As one cohort member noted, "The program is a marvelous experience. It's too bad that it has to come to an end."

Payoffs for Site Supervisors

The mentor selection process is comprehensive and challenging. Therefore, once included, mentors experience a feeling of professional recognition that is not easily gained in other ways by school administrators. There is a feeling of pride in being associated with the program, which is supportive of the notion that extrinsic rewards, such as pay for services performed, are not high on the motivational scale of most site supervisors. They also appreciate being kept up-to-date about ideas and skills in educational administration. Further, mentors mention the extreme value gained from being challenged by interns regarding their logic and how they act on that logic. As one mentor noted, she appreciates getting the chance to "get clearer and more structured about what I'm about." This opportunity to reflect on practice is viewed as critically important but not widely available to them. They also note that, due to the program's emphasis on hands-on learning, they value having talented individuals at their schools for a few months to share the load. Finally, they find it very satisfactory to have an influence on the coming generation of educational leaders and to help interns become an important part of that future.

Payoffs for School Districts

School districts in the Puget Sound region are sensitive to the fact that many of the current group of educational administrators will soon be retiring. There is a unique opportunity to replace them with entry-level administrators who can lead the schools into the next century. Districts are also aware that a different kind of preparation is required if that is to happen. Therefore, they were quite receptive to the area's request to help them bring about necessary program changes. Their commitment of funds to support release time for internships; their willingness to serve on planning, curriculum, and selection committees; and their subsequent interest in hiring program graduates are clear indicators of their concern. In the effort, they also come into more frequent and meaningful contact with university faculty members, to the point that a real sense of partnership is becoming deeply embedded.

Payoffs for the University/College of Education/Leadership Area

The University of Washington is a major research institute, but it has a relatively small emphasis on education, at least as judged by the number of faculty and students in the college. Except for one article in *University Week*, a faculty and staff newsletter, there has been no evidence of university recognition of the program, let alone appreciation of the ways it supports institutional goals. At the college level, the recognition is much clearer. The current dean is concerned about the preparation of educational leaders and feels that the area is making the right decision in institutionalizing the Danforth program. In fact, as noted, he is willing to commit part of the college's shrinking resource base to support the effort. He also recognizes the importance of the goodwill that the program creates with the region's school districts, goodwill that helps to establish an image of the college as being relevant and concerned about the problems these districts are confronting.

There are also indications of meaningful spill-overs into other areas of the college. For example, a faculty member from Teacher Education, who was involved in the planning for the Danforth program, has instituted cohorts, instructional units instead of formal courses, and field experiences in the Professional Development Center for middle schools, which she runs.

For the area, the most obvious payoff is the development of a new program, which is judged to be much better than its traditional, and soon to be phased out, program. It also has spill-over effects, such as increased opportunities for the faculty to develop closer ties with the field, through regular field-supervision interactions with mentors and through attendance at program-sponsored events. Further, it promotes a healthy balance between teaching a body of knowledge from the behavioral sciences and learning through reflective/inductive reasoning. Finally, it provides guidance, as the area reexamines its other programs. For example, plans for the superintendent program include cohorts, structured field experiences, integration of field experiences with academic curriculum, and reflective seminars once a month for a half day. The doctoral program is also going through an evolutionary change. Already in place this year are activities that include core learning elements, such as leadership as a moral endeavor, the dynamics of educational organizations, perspectives on policy and policy making in education, team teaching, reflective seminars, and field experiences that are appropriate at this advanced preparation level.

ONGOING ISSUES

Great strides have been made in a relatively short time, but there are still issues that must be resolved if the program is to live up to its potential. Fortunately, the Program Design Committee, the curriculum committees, and the larger faculty group are aware of this fact. Equally important, norms that emphasize evaluation, positive criticism, and willingness to make changes as needed are well established. What this amounts to is a perspective of the program as a living system that will languish and perish if it does not continue to grow.

Academic Program

Several additional program elements may be worth considering. First, currently, there is little emphasis on technological applications for management and instruction. This is a serious shortcoming, given the increasing applications of technology in school settings generally, as well as the high technological profile of the region specifically. Second, students would benefit from a continued focus throughout the academic year on the intensive group dynamics that occur under the guidance of the organization-development specialists in the

10-day residential session. As they gain clinical experience and acquire deeper understandings about organizational dynamics, cohort members reach a state of readiness for further process learnings that center on group and organizational facilitation skills. Additional organization-development opportunities would positively affect cohort members' leadership capacities. Third, the program remains relatively isolated from the vast human resources that exist in academic disciplines across the university. Promoting inputs in planning and delivery of instruction by faculty from areas such as public health and public affairs might be a powerful and logical extension of the area's desire to partner with resource persons who have something to offer to the program.

There is also a need to maintain vigilance to ensure that a proper balance is maintained in program development and delivery. In this regard, the effort to integrate clinical and academic experiences will require constant attention. The present coordinator oversees the process of integration, but she will be leaving in a year. The area will have to develop a system to ensure that integration will continue regardless of who replaces her *before* she leaves so that there is adequate time for a smooth transition. In similar fashion, the balance between academic rigor and interpersonal and group dynamics should be maintained. In moving from a traditional academic program that focused on content, often delivered in a didactic mode, to a program that emphasizes reflection and affective elements, it would not be difficult for the pendulum to swing too far and create a new imbalance. This has not yet happened, but the positive sense that pervades the program could lead to such an imbalance if the faculty does not remain vigilant.

As the program is institutionalized, there is a need to guard the preservation of the intent and content of this innovative program. Presently, the program is being micromanaged by the chairperson and the coordinator. Other faculty members are involved in one way or another, but their levels of commitment and support vary. Enthusiasm will probably increase over time, as positive program outcomes build up and as faculty vacancies are filled (assuming that they will be and that candidates are hired who support the philosophy of the program), but during the transition, efforts should be made to encourage faculty commitment and support.

In addition, whereas the area was able to capture much of students' tuition payments for program purposes, this will cease with full institutionalization. Those in key positions, such as the college dean, will have to be relied on to make up for this significant loss. In short, without careful tending, the very success of an innovative program can lead to its demise if institutionalization requires compromising purposes and access to resources in order to gain acceptance by the system.

Recruitment and Admissions

Admissions has been limited to a highly selected and limited size of cohort. This may be viewed as inappropriate for an institution of public higher education. However, candidates who do not meet the area's criteria can still seek admissions in one of the other public preparation programs in the region (e.g., Seattle University, Seattle Pacific University, and a branch of Western Washington in Seattle, or Puget Sound University in Tacoma).

The recruitment and admissions process works, in that fine candidates are identified, persevere, and move into administrative positions. Still, there are things that can be done to improve the structure:

1. The area presently makes presentations about the program to school officials and then relies on them to advertise its availability and provide whatever orientation that may occur to help individuals decide whether to apply for nomination and admissions. First, an orientation session planned for potential students and conducted by the area would help ensure that program expectations and demands are clearly understood. Second, the process is highly collaborative, in that many district practitioners are involved in the selection process, but final decisions are made by area faculty members. The collaborative partnership approach that has been established should encourage the faculty to consider practitioner input at the final selection stage.

2. There is need to expand beyond the present admissions data base, which is limited to traditional academic-oriented infor-

mation, with the exception of statements about values, to include means of gathering leadership-related data that are behaviorally anchored. For example, an assessment center might be considered as part of the admissions process.

3. University norms and bureaucratic rules may jeopardize the program. For example, university programs are student-credit-hour driven, but the area has chosen to phase out its traditional program and to keep entry-level certification admissions down to a maximum of 20 new students each year. If the university becomes concerned about producing student credit hours, either special dispensations will have to be granted, or student-credit-hour differences will have to be made up in other ways.

4. Whereas the faculty could formerly process admissions relatively easily because the Danforth program was viewed to be experimental, in the future, they will probably have to go through standard university channels and follow established rules. Unless the area develops creative responses to this ingrained system, university rules may seriously compromise several program biases, including the encouragement of racial, ethnic, and gender diversity.

Internships

A solid approach that ensures high-quality experiences and extensive time-on-task has led to internship experiences that are meaningful. Several changes could make them even better. First, because of the emphasis on hands on learning, students do not get many planned opportunities to shadow administrators and learn by observation before they are put into a series of high-involvement experiences. A brief period of shadowing each of their three site mentors would let them focus on those leaders' styles and high-priority actions and would let them expand on their own limited repertoires. It would also give them a chance to become acquainted with the dynamics of their internship sites before having to play a leadership role in them.

Second, although it is important to involve faculty members in the program, particularly in the clinical portion, so that they can more fully understand the need to integrate campus experiences with field experiences, it is questionable that heavy involvement in field supervision is an effective way of doing this. Faculty members either have never been school administrators, or they had this experience long ago. As such, they may find it difficult to provide the insights and guidance necessary in the role of field supervisor. In addition, this activity is awarded by reduced teaching loads, taking them away from their central function, a function that they probably perform more effectively than their field supervision role. At best, this involvement should be examined so that it is employed with maximum positive impact for all involved parties. If it is important, then adequate training needs to be provided. If it is not, then outstanding administrators should be hired to be field supervisors.

Finally, because the program philosophy includes an expectation of alternative and diverse internship experiences, three ideas might be considered. First, most cohort members come from urban and suburban school districts, so it might be appropriate for them to have one of their internship experiences in a rural school system. Second, nonschool sites (e.g., business and government) might be considered as alternative experiences to broaden cohort members' perspectives, particularly since interagency cooperation efforts are likely to become increasingly relevant for school effectiveness. Third, planned opportunities to become acquainted with districtwide dynamics should be included as part of the field experience. For example, observations of school-board meetings and visits to district support centers such as cafeteria, personnel, and business offices would give interns a more comprehensive perspective of educational systems.

Placement

As measured by placement, the program is effective. School districts invest resources in their selected candidate's programs (paying for release time and occasionally for other program-related expenses), so there is more likelihood that they will seek to hire them.

This can also be a problem. There is an expectation on the part of two of these districts that graduates will return in one professional role or another for up to 2 years. Some of these candidates have been offered positions in other districts, which is cause for concern finan-

cially, both to them and to their home school districts. Current understandings may need to be reviewed and modified as appropriate.

Financing

The area has been very creative in identifying and securing a solid
financial base for the program, including securing Danforth funds,
getting districts to commit resources for release time, having students
support the residential session, getting tuition returns by using continuing education for certification students, and finding small grant
sources for related needs. However, unless the college commits resources, it will be difficult to institutionalize the program. Specifically,
the college needs to secure sufficient funds for full funding of the
coordinator's line and for ongoing program support needs such as
secretarial help, field supervision, and adjunct instructors.

Partnering

Collaborative partnerships, which form a basic value of the program, occur in a variety of ways, including planning, curriculum
development, mentor selection, and program evaluation. To keep the
partnership vital as conditions change, the area must continually add
new members. In this regard, the mentor pool has to be evaluated,
purged as necessary, and enriched by adding newly identified leaders; new districts need to be approached as partners to reduce de-
pendency on a small number of districts and to avoid the likelihood
that a favored few will take on the shape of an elite club; and a
newsletter should be considered for dissemination to the mentor
pool (some of whom feel isolated from the program when they do not
work with an intern), school-district supporters, alumni, and current
students.

Coordination

As noted, the current coordinator, who has been with the program
since its inception, will be leaving very soon. Her departure will cause
some discomfort and possibly discontinuity unless her successor is
selected quite carefully. This means that clear criteria have to be

identified, an attractive salary level has to be agreed on and secured from the university, and highly qualified candidates have to be encouraged to apply for the position. If the position is identified as a tenure-track line, careful thought has to be given to productivity expectations and ways of rewarding the new coordinator for attending to the demands of the job. Further, coordinating activities associated with the program appear to be more than one person can adequately manage, particularly because the program has grown both in complexity and the number of cohort members. At present, the program's continuing excellence is highly dependent on the current coordinator's extraordinary energy level and willingness to work very long days. Secretarial support is needed, as is funding for field supervision unless full-time faculty continue to serve in this role.

In Closing

The University of Washington's efforts demonstrate the clear need to be responsive to changing environments, even if that means dismantling a well-established and positively perceived program. The faculty recognized that the reform movement that dominated the 1980s was creating enormous pressure for school districts to do business in a radically different way. As the major preparer of leaders for the region's school systems, the faculty took on the commitment to work in collaboration with school-district leaders to challenge its existing program approach and to take the risks required to reinvent itself.

Learnings Across the Terrain

The experimental programs being tested at universities in cooperation with the Danforth Foundation are leading to better understandings of what is required to improve the preparation of educational administrators, and particularly of school principals. What began as a limited project in 1987 at four universities has grown to become a nationally important activity that has directly involved 22 universities, and less directly, many others have become interested observers of the effort.

The intent of this chapter is to highlight learnings gained through case studies of the experimental programs being conducted at the University of Alabama, the University of Central Florida, the University of Connecticut, California State University at Fresno, and the University of Washington. The focus is on identifying effective responses to the preparation of educational leaders that may be of help to other universities examining ways of increasing the effectiveness of their preparation for educational leaders. Included in the discussion are 10 topics: the dynamics of program change; student recruitment, selection, and learning needs; academic offerings; internships; cohorts; program management and coordination: required resources; issues related to institutionalization; a comparison of these Danforth-related programs with more traditional programs; and implications for the future of administrator preparation.

The Dynamics of Program Change

Trying to change significantly programs for the preparation of educational leaders is a hazardous business at best. There are many pitfalls that must be avoided and coalitions that must be developed, to create sufficient momentum for such programs to survive long enough to have a fair chance of being institutionalized. The effort is doubly complicated by the fact that most traditional programs are deeply entrenched. Those who have developed and maintained these programs are not usually enthusiastic about reconceptualizing and restructuring them.

How experimental programs are established is as important as the quality of the structures and the content that are implemented. The effort to create readiness and support for the new programs at the five universities varied. At the University of Alabama, studies indicating a high retirement rate among the state's educational administrators, along with the faculty's sensitivity to the national criticism of preparation programs, led to an increase in readiness to examine the status-quo program and a commitment to make changes, as appropriate. The faculty's efforts to seek the advice and involvement of superintendents and principals, as well as the creativity and guidance of the former chairperson who initiated and established the program, extended the readiness for meaningful change.

There are clear indicators of the goodwill and support that have been built by these coordinators and the faculty. The two coordinators who guided the program through its first 5 years were senior faculty members whose vision, sense of mission, attention to task, extensive administrative experience, and well-earned positive reputations among school leaders were significant factors in getting the program off the ground. The faculty, sensitive to the need to develop and maintain effective partnerships with educational leaders across the state, established an advisory committee system to seek inputs and sponsorship. They also affected the political system, gaining permission from the state's department of education to run a pilot program and later having the program institutionalized as the state's approach to certification.

Several critical aspects created a readiness for experimentation and risk taking at the University of Central Florida. These include a university that is relatively new, where traditions are not deeply embedded; a national environment pressing for educational reform; a surrounding community growing rapidly and changing in demographic composition; a new leader, the doctoral program director, who brought a new vision regarding leadership preparation with him; and a cooperative faculty that did not have a commitment or stake in the status-quo program, took pleasure in associating with each other, and included several relatively new members. It was in this fertile environment that the new program took root.

Even with this positive set of circumstances, the program could have floundered when the initial coordinator left the scene. It did not because the doctoral director, who had conceived the original program design, stepped forward to manage the program and encourage its participants, thus keeping it on track. Similarly, the initial coordinator's replacement is a tireless champion of the program.

Together, the doctoral director and the new coordinator made a strong team because of their commitment to the program and because of their skills and connections. The doctoral director protected the fledgling program within the complex organizational framework of the university, while the new faculty member took full advantage of her extensive working knowledge of the local education community and the respect she had as an administrator in that community.

At the California State University at Fresno, the coordinator, working alone, sought out allies in the field and, with them, developed a set of expectations and a common language, initiated a series of ongoing meetings with them, and worked at expanding their numbers prior to initiating the program. Local superintendents view the coordinator as a "Pied Piper," someone who gets out front, has a powerful message, has the ability to present it clearly, and is able to attract others to join him in a visionary adventure.

At the University of Washington, there was already a sense of urgency about the need to change the preparation program, even though it had just been the recipient of a prestigious award. In fact, the chairperson and some of the faculty were in the vanguard of the critics. Further, a forum existed, in the form of the Puget Sound Educational Consortium, for broad exploration of related issues. It was not long before ideas crystallized as like-minded key educational leaders took the opportunity to share their concerns and to explore ways of bringing about meaningful change.

A small cadre of change agents seized the opportunity to develop an overall vision, enlist key players, and secure both national funding and local resource commitments. The former chairperson had significant status in the educational community, a positive attitude about needed changes, a willingness to confront status-quo thinking, and the connections necessary to obtain start-up resources. The coordinator has a rich experiential base as an educational administrator, a clear vision of what is required to provide meaningful leadership preparation, and boundless energy to establish, maintain, and improve the program. The current chairperson engaged in the dialogue since the inception of the program, initially as an interested faculty member who was in agreement with the basic values and structure of the program. As chairperson, he has nurtured and supported the program through his teaching, innovative redesign ideas, commitment to program evaluation, critical inquiry, and the development of arguments for more extensive university resource commitments. Each of these champions pursued their unique roles with tenacity and persuasiveness.

In contrast to the other four settings, the program at the University of Connecticut was initiated before adequate readiness was developed. As a result, the program was deferred for a year. When it was finally launched in 1990, there were only four participants. It was not until 1991 that a full cohort was recruited for the program. Realistically, in this case, there may have been no other choice but to risk a premature start-up because waiting for readiness to develop may have been futile. The planners had to risk going ahead in hopes that a felt need would emerge, along with a willingness to become involved in the effort. At the outset, this meant that the concern for change was limited to the outgoing dean and associate dean, who were returning to a rather traditional leadership-preparation program. It took some time for the faculty to accept and commit itself to the suggested program changes. Similarly, although there were leaders in a few school districts who had been involved in discussions about the need to improve leadership preparation, many others had not been part of the debate.

Certainly there were real constraints, such as lack of school-district funds for release time, but such difficulties and resource limitations always exist. If a greater sense of need existed at the outset and a willingness to take risks and redefine priorities were established, these problems might not have been viewed as such major roadblocks.

Fortunately, key influential persons played important roles from the outset. The outgoing associate dean recognized the importance of changing the department's preparation program; the outgoing dean encouraged the department to apply for Danforth program funds and appoint one of its members as a coordinator to establish the program. The dean continued to play a key role in the hiring of the current coordinator and has supported her through his extensive network of relations with educational leaders across the state. The current coordinator is enthusiastic about her assignment and has introduced many improvements in the program. In addition, several district-level educational leaders and school site administrators have been involved in planning activities from the outset.

READINESS: CRITICAL ELEMENTS

The experiences of these universities highlight three important lessons regarding the dynamics of program change:

1. Readiness is a necessary foundation on which to create new programs. Readiness requires that there be some doubt about the appropriateness or effectiveness of current efforts. This doubt may be based on any number of considerations—for example, as a response to the national reform agenda; feedback from students, alumni, or school district and site-based leaders; discussions about the high rate of retirement among current educational administrators; and the changing leadership requirements for our schools in the future. Whatever the specific concerns are, the important thing is to trigger the dialogue and foster an interest in change. Without a sense of

need, there is little likelihood that the necessary energy and willingness to take risks will be generated.

2. Program champions are necessary to guide the process. Changing the status quo requires finding individuals who are firm believers and effective organizers, and who have the commitment and energy around which others can coalesce. These individuals must have the vision to see how results can be better for program graduates, school districts, and the university, if the changes are implemented. They must also have the skills necessary to guide the effort through the thorny thickets of university and school-district bureaucracies and the status to get others to join them in the effort. Such individuals must be recruited if they are not already available. If more than one champion can be identified, all the better, because different program-change activities require different interests and talents. Furthermore, being a change agent can be a lonely business—having someone to work with can be quite important for the well-being of those involved and for the positive outcomes that can accrue for the program.

3. Partnerships are vital. Key influential persons must be recruited to become participants and sponsors. These role players include chairpersons and deans in the university who make decisions about the use of time and the allocation of resources; faculty members who must modify their teaching and advisement behaviors; superintendents and other central-office personnel who make decisions about district and candidate participation, as well as about release time for internships and the eventual placement of graduates; and site-based administrators who must nominate program participants, arrange for classroom coverage, and act as mentors for interns. These groups play critical roles in the program. They must have a common understanding of purposes and processes for the program to succeed. For this to happen, there must be a forum for dialogue in which all role players come together as equal partners to create a common vision, agree on strategies to achieve that vision, and share a firm belief that the effort will be of benefit to all parties involved. Readiness for change

requires that coalitions be developed and that a basic philosophy and guiding principles for program development are
open to debate so that they will be clear, comprehensive, and
shared.

The groundwork for change must be laid effectively before even
the best conceived program is initiated. Development of sensitivity,
understanding, motivation, and the willingness to take risks and
remain flexible during the tentative early stages of change is dependent on the creation of a high level of readiness for change.

Student Recruitment, Selection,
and Learning Needs

the universities included in the review have made major efforts
to change the ground rules regarding who participates in preparation
programs. All are consciously moving away from the traditional
approach, which is based on candidate self-selection and emphasizes
academic potential but does not place much emphasis on leadership
potential. All five of the universities require school-district leader
nominations before candidates are considered for admissions. Three
expect the districts to screen applicants before submitting nominations for admissions. These are major changes from the typical walk-
in, self-selected admissions candidate system that currently prevails
at most universities (see Table 8.1).

The modified selection process rests on several assumptions.
First, field leaders will nominate based on knowledge of candidates'
potential to become educational leaders. Second, if they make these
difficult nomination decisions, they are more likely to become sponsors, helping candidates to obtain release time and other resources
required to complete the program successfully. Third, field leaders
who nominate individuals and help them move through programs of
study are more likely to be inclined to hire them or at least to help
them find administrative positions than would be true if they had no
such stake in the candidates.

Of those admitted, the male/female ratio approximates that of
most other preparation programs, with females far outnumbering

males. Racial and ethnic minority enrollments are improving, due, in large part, to purposeful recruitment. School-district leaders are encouraged to seek out qualified minority candidates. Such positive recognition by established school-district leaders is often sufficient impetus to cause such individuals to consider this option.

Admissions processes appear to be going through a transition, from an exclusive emphasis on academic potential to inclusion of an emphasis on leadership potential. All five of the universities require nominations by superintendents and/or principals. Three have added essays on leadership, and two include an interview that focuses on leadership and values. Although several other Danforth-related programs do gather behaviorally anchored information, such as the information provided by assessment centers, none of the five case-study settings have done so.

The pool of candidates is relatively high, varying from two to five times the numbers accepted for admissions, with the exception of Fresno, which currently takes all qualified applicants nominated by district superintendents. On the output end, results are less clear, with three institutions' graduates doing quite well in finding positions and two institutions' graduates not being very successful in this effort. In both situations, there are extenuating circumstances—the University of Connecticut has only a few graduates at this point, and the University of Central Florida's graduates have encountered a severe budgetary problem that is causing school districts to reduce their administrative overhead rather than consider hiring new administrators.

Finally, depending on state-licensure requirements, the type of programs offered vary. In California, Florida, and Washington, a master's degree can be earned while obtaining administrative certification. In Alabama, teachers are expected to have obtained a master's degree in their area of preparation, while in Connecticut, most teachers come to the program with a master's and work to obtain a sixth-year diploma, as well as administrative certification. Such variations are to be expected, given the fact that each state sets its own rules for professional licensure.

(Text continued on p. 188)

TABLE 8.1 Program Participants

| | Recruitment | Approximate selection ratio | Cohort demographics | | | | Admissions process | Type of program | Placement |
			Male	Female	Majority	Minority			
Alabama	Superintendent and principal nominations	1 of 5 applicants	22%	78%	75%	25%	Traditional plus essay on educational leadership	Nondegree (certification only)	5 yrs = 70% estimate
Central Florida	Principals nominate District screening committee	1 of 5 applicants	15%	85%	72%	28%	Traditional	Master's	1 year = 11%
Connecticut	Principals nominate Districts encouraged to screen nominees	1 of 3 applicants	32%	68%	79%	21%	Traditional plus; 1. Recommendations from a peer teacher and a district administrator. 2. An interview with a committee of field administrators and university faculty members to establish motivation and leadership potential	Nondegree (certification + 6th-year diploma program)	1 year = 1 of 4 (25%)

Fresno	Superintendents nominate	All who qualify	32%	68%	67%	33%	Traditional	Master's or certification	1 year = 67%
Washington	Most nominated by principals and screened by district committees; a few self-identified	1 of 2 applicants	37%	63%	71%	29%	Traditional plus; 1. Recommendations from principal, a teacher the principal chooses, and one the candidate selects. 2. An interview with field leaders and university faculty to clarify values about leadership. 3. An essay on leadership under changing conditions	Master's or certification	4 years = 72%

STUDENTS: CRITICAL ELEMENTS

The efforts made to control who participates in preparation pro-grams are changing the composition of student groups. Important shifts in emphasis include the following:

1. Purposeful selection increases the likelihood of identifying candidates with high potential, both academically and as future leaders in education. Educational leadership has much to learn from other professionals, such as medicine and law, both of which understand the importance of controlling en-trance to their fields. Besides promoting a better selection process, it promotes identification of more racial and ethnic minority candidates and encourages shared responsibility as school-district leaders, site administrators, and university fac-ulty members cooperate to manage the nomination process.

2. Admissions processes are in need of review and change. Tra-ditionally, the emphasis has been on academic potential (e.g., nationally normed tests, transcripts to ascertain grade-point averages, and recommendations that tend to focus on the likelihood of completing a program of studies). These criteria are useful to establish the candidates' potential as students, but they are not particularly helpful in establishing their potential as leaders. The ability to absorb and recall knowledge is im-portant, but the more important intent of preparation is to produce leaders, not scholars. Leaders are measured by their sense of purpose, ability to get others engaged with them as they translate purposes, manage the enterprise, and intervene when required to keep the system on target. These are qualities that are best measured by past leadership behaviors, the exis-tence of an educational platform that can be exhibited through a clear communication of purposes, and demonstration of the ability to respond adequately in situations that require leader-ship behaviors.

3. Responsibility for placement has traditionally been left to individual graduates. There has been little effort to guide the process on the part of those preparing these candidates. Closer working relationships among school-district leaders, site ad-ministrators, and university faculty members are beginning to

change this situation. A sponsorship system is beginning to evolve, and, with it, a much better placement record for program graduates is beginning to emerge. Nomination and selection to participate in preparation programs is the first step toward controlling entrance to the profession. Effective preparation is the second step. Purposeful involvement in the placement process is the third step.

Academic Offerings

Effective preparation programs require academic programs that can meet the emerging needs of educational leaders who are being asked to be facilitators, instructional leaders, and team managers. Recognizing this, some universities are working at redefining academic content and delivery in their preparation programs, but in most cases, not to the extent that they are improving the quality of internships. This is not surprising, given that academic programs were already in place at these institutions, while the internship component had to be created or drastically changed. The complexity of the task and the limited time available may encourage planners to focus on relative vacuums first, but changes and improvements in the field component of programs must be matched by changes and improvements in academic content and delivery.

The University of Alabama has designed an academic program that is unique in content and delivery. The content is centered on knowledge and skills required for entry-level administrative positions. Originally defined as managerial "survival skills," more recently, the content has been modified to include a focus on instructional leadership. Academic content is organized in modules, most of which are 2 hours in duration, over a 10-week period in the first summer of the program. Instructors include faculty from the leadership area, other faculty from across the campus who are specialists in areas included in the curriculum, and practicing administrators known for their interest and experience in specific content areas. Integrating seminars are held every 2 weeks to help students synthesize the content, and "bridging" classes are planned for a week during the fall and spring semesters as a follow-up to summer learnings. The program is evaluated in a number of ways. Each module is reviewed prior to presentation, students evaluate modules daily, and an annual evaluation is conducted by doctoral students.

Academic offerings at the University of Central Florida are typical of those found elsewhere. Courses focus on foundations, curriculum, management, supervision, law, finance, and instruction. Within courses, modifications are being introduced, including simulations, case studies, role playing, and reflective writing. Site-based assignments are being made to bring campus seminars and internship experiences closer together. Most important, the Renaissance strand, which is extracurricular, exposes students to alternative ideas and to different cultures. In the process, it is helping them to broaden their perspectives about the purposes and strategies of educational leadership.

The program is evaluated several ways—through a review of student portfolios, feedback by alumni, and an ongoing evaluation project being conducted by a professor of instruction in the college. Evaluation and feedback have been used to change the program sequence and the time for completion of it, and to increase field-based exercises.

Academic content at the University of Connecticut focuses on administration, program development, supervision, staff development, the principalship, learning, and law. Changes thus far center on attempts to sequence learnings, engage leading practitioners to team teach with faculty members in order to balance theory and concepts with experience and practice. Attempts are also being made to unbundle courses and to present content as learning modules, and to introduce long-term field-based projects so that students can experience planning and leadership activities. Evaluation is conducted through discussions held by the coordinator with faculty, students, and district sponsors, and also through the expectation that students will provide feedback at the end of each class period.

California State University at Fresno has sequenced academic experiences, focusing on instructional leadership and emphasizing hands-on participative learning. Academic credit is given for workshops designed around topics of interest identified by students. An advisory committee system ensures high involvement by leading practitioners in the design of academic content. Evaluation comes in the form of feedback by superintendents, students in classes, and faculty monitoring of the overall program.

The University of Washington initially developed working assumptions regarding equity and excellence, leadership, organizational change, collaboration, inquiry, and reflective practice, as foundations for program development. Curriculum design committees composed of faculty members, field leaders, students, and alumni meet to establish the content, instructional design, and sequence of academic content. Extensive coordination, networking, and flexibility are required because academic content (which is organized around two major themes—Moral Dimensions of Leadership and Inquiry, Organizations, and Educational Change—rather than around courses) is delivered when school-district dynamics are likely to parallel academic content. Instruction, which is delivered by faculty members and leading practitioners, occurs during the daytime on Thursdays and Saturdays. Meeting during the morning and afternoon enhances the ability of students to absorb the content. Evaluation is a deeply embedded value. Every 3 months, those involved with instruction come together to share their perceptions about the program and to receive student feedback, which is collected regularly by the coordinator.

ACADEMIC OFFERINGS: CRITICAL ELEMENTS

Each of the five universities has made efforts to change and improve the academic content of its preparation program. Variations across programs reflect differences in environmental situations, program longevity, the extent to which efforts to change have been balanced between internship enrichment and academic content change, and purposeful evaluation. The outcomes of their efforts have implications for other preparation programs:

1. The academic content of preparation programs must emphasize the skills and knowledge that are required in the roles for which students are preparing. This can only happen if faculty members are willing to examine current programs, eliminate content that is not directly relevant, and reduce time given to

content that can be appropriately modified. Faculty must also create new content after they become knowledgeable about the roles and activities that novice administrators are likely to encounter when they complete preparation programs.

2. The delivery of academic content must change in ways that increase the potential for learning. They must also role model better ways of delivering instruction in schools. Included in this effort is the need to break out of the set course mentality (i.e., three credits for 45 semester hours equals a course); exploring alternatives such as units and modules; capitalizing on what is known about adult learning by promoting interactive learning and reducing the emphasis on didactic/lecturing approaches; tapping the wealth of instructional talent that is available in other units of the university and among educational administrators in the field; experimenting with different time blocks—from less than an hour to multiple hours—and times of the day for delivery of instruction to maximize readiness to learn; and exploring alternative locations for instruction that are more accessible and that capitalize on the learnings that can be obtained at these sites.

3. Evaluation, both formative and summative, needs to be conducted, to encourage incremental improvements of academic content and delivery of instruction. Changes that will be required to respond to the demands for reform call for ongoing evaluations of efforts.

No longer can preparation programs be viewed in a static way. Rather, it is more appropriate to think of them as living organisms. The need for change will be constant, if preparation programs are expected to survive and thrive. Serious review and revamping of preparation content and instructional delivery is long past due. Sacred cows must be challenged, particularly given the rapid rate of societal change and the demand for comparable change in our school systems. Those charged with preparation of tomorrow's educational leaders must be willing to be critical of their current efforts and ready to make the changes that are needed.

Internships

The establishment of a more structured set of field experiences for future educational administrators is centrally important to the entire program redesign effort. In particular, efforts must be made to increase the quality of the experience and the time-on-task for the clinical component of the program.

Each of the five universities has developed a handbook or manual to guide the internship experience. However, as the brief descriptions of the internship structure at the five universities depicted in Table 8.2 indicate, there is no simple formula, particularly given the different contingencies that exist at each location.

Besides overall facilitation by the coordinator, direct internship supervision is conducted by two role players—site managers (usually principals) who are encouraged to act as mentors, and field supervisors who provide guidance and support and monitor the mentor/intern relationship. The interns' experiences are greatly affected by the quality of supervision provided by these two individuals.

In all five cases, field supervisors are university professors. There is a logic to their being involved in the program. It helps them become sensitive to the needs of students and encourages them to gear their teaching and program advisement to meet these needs. However, many of them have never been school administrators. Even those who have, have typically not been in school leadership positions for some time. It is questionable that, as a group, they can be as effective in this role as school-based administrators with extensive experience and positive reputations as leaders. Further, field supervision, whether it includes load credit or not, inevitably cuts into the time faculty members need to devote to teaching and research.

Relations with mentors are identified with regularity by program participants as the most important element in their development as educational leaders. All five institutions refer to site supervisors as mentors, and each is trying to ensure that the role is more extensive than that which is typically expected of site supervisors. Beyond supervision, mentors, as the more experienced partners in the

(Text continued on p. 196)

TABLE 8.2 Internship Information

	Where	Time	When	Guidelines/ activities	Supervision	Opportunities for reflection
Alabama	At candidate's school	300-500 hours	1 week before and 1 week after school term; the rest by arrangement with mentor	Detailed manual to guide internship activities and evaluation	University faculty as field supervisors, who visit sites a few times; mentors are principals from interns' schools	Presently 4 Saturdays a year; adding a "bridging class" 1 week in fall and spring
Central Florida	In own district but not own school; 2 experiences at different levels; 1 must be at a site at least 20% different in demographics from own school	Was 35 days, now 24 days	Was 15 days during school term and 20 in summer; now 12 days in each of 2 summers	General manual with state competencies to guide activities and evaluation	University faculty as field supervisors; mentors nominated by school district and selected by coordinator	Only during regular classes or when coordinator calls group together (e.g., ½ hour before class or on a Saturday at her home)
Connecticut	Outside own district; 1 experience, unless mentor arranges for alternative summer experiences	90 days	15 days in Fall, 15 days in spring, 30 days in each of 2 summers	Handbook with general role expectations and evaluation guidelines; Interns set own goals	University faculty as field supervisors who visit sites 4 times; mentors nominated by school districts and selected from a mentor pool by the coordinator	Once per month

Fresno	Assigned by superintendent	Is 1500 hours, will be 150 hours	Is during school year; will be during the summer	Guidebook with desired competencies and how to evaluate them	University faculty as field supervisors, who visit sites 2 times per semester; mentors selected by superintendents	Only in required classes
Washington	3 experiences, 2 must be outside district; students find sites from established mentor pool	Minimum of ½ time for a year or 700 hours; some get full time, or 1400 hours	During school year	Handbook defining mentor/intern roles, activities, and evaluation	University faculty member as field supervisors; mentors nominated by school district and selected from a mentor pool by the coordinator	Weekly

arrangement, are encouraged to develop close, caring, and ongoing relationships with interns.

When the relationship develops as intended, mentors provide leadership opportunities, give feedback for growth, offer a sympathetic ear for the inevitable questions and concerns that arise, and act as role models to be emulated. However, for the relationship to be effective, three things must exist. First, a system must be established that includes mentor nominations by highly reputable field-based leaders and includes review and selection by university faculty members who know the field. Second, because mentoring is a unique activity, training must be provided to clarify role expectations and provision of ongoing support and feedback as the relationship develops. Third, an evaluation system must be established to ascertain whether mentors are providing the support that interns require. Mentors who are not may need corrective feedback or may even have to be removed from the mentor pool.

Extrinsic rewards for mentors are minimal, although there are some efforts to provide rewards such as library privileges and invitations to join students and alumni at various kinds of learning sessions. However, mentors do receive important intrinsic rewards. They receive the opportunity to reflect on their leadership behaviors and decisions as they explain what they do to interns. They also receive the opportunity to catch up on the latest thinking about educational administration as they listen to interns talk about their reading and classroom experiences. Most important, they receive the chance to directly influence the next generation of educational leaders. This is a special privilege and a rewarding activity for many midcareer administrators.

In short, it should be recognized that mentoring provides unique professional development opportunities for site-based leaders. In fact, when the mentor relationship works well, it appears to be as important to the mentor as it is to the intern. These positive outcomes have not typically been given much consideration in field-based preparation programs.

Concerning specifics about each of the universities, students at the University of Alabama serve 300- to 500-hour internships at their own schools. School districts originally agreed to provide funds for a semester-long full-time internship. However, severe budget cuts at the state level caused them to withdraw this support, thus reducing the release time available for internships, changing the field-based experience to a week before and after school, with the rest coming as a result of negotiations between interns and mentors. Quality of supervision varies, depending on interest and abilities of specific mentors. The opportunity to learn from field-based experiences is also limited by the fact that field supervisors visit each site only two or three times a year and, until the present, there have only been 4 days during the academic year for interns to come together for reflection. Reflection is being enhanced by a bridging class that will meet for a full week during the fall and spring semesters.

Students at Central Florida University originally received 35 days of internship, 15 of which were during the school year. Due to severe fiscal problems being confronted by Florida school districts, the number of internship days has been reduced to 24, all of which occur in the summer months. Students' internships are in their own school districts, but not at their own schools. They are required to have experiences at two different school levels, both of which are under the guidance of mentors nominated by the central office. At least one site must be demographically different from their own. Other than time arranged by the coordinator, there are no regular opportunities for interns, as a group, to reflect on field experiences.

A single internship experience of 90 days outside the student's home school district is the norm at the University of Connecticut. Fifteen days are provided during each of two school years, and 30 days are provided during each of two summers. Many students supplement district release time by taking personal leave days to create more internship time during the school year. Sites and mentors come from a pool nominated by leaders of participating school districts. Students maintain journals and reflective seminars are held monthly.

Superintendents from participating school districts play a central role in the internship process at California State University at Fresno. They select interns' sites and mentors and act as secondary mentors for interns. District resources were sufficient to permit full-time internships during the school year, but with lack of funds, field-based programs will be moved exclusively into the summer months. Further, the time-on-task, which has been 1500 hours, may be reduced to only 150 hours as the program is institutionalized. Group reflection on experience occurs, but only through regularly scheduled courses.

The University of Washington requires three different internship experiences over the school year. Two of these must be outside the student's school district. At minimum, internships are half-time over the year, but where resources are available, full-time internships are encouraged. A mentor pool, based on nominations by field-based leaders, is reviewed by students who prioritize their preferences and then set up interviews with potential mentors for internship positions. Journals are maintained, and reflective seminars are held weekly.

INTERNSHIPS: CRITICAL ELEMENTS

Reorienting preparation programs toward more emphasis on field-based experiences has been a major challenge for these universities. There are four areas in particular that have direct implications for other universities seeking to move in this direction:

1. Effective internship experiences require sufficient time-on-task in challenging situations. Thus far, it has been extremely difficult to secure the time needed during the school year, when students are in attendance, for program participants to get the field experiences they need to learn the leadership roles for which they are preparing. Resources must be obtained in order to provide adequate release time for this activity. Without sufficient time-on-task, interns cannot shift their thinking from teacher to administrator, gain a clear perception of the role requirements of site-based leadership, or gain the skills and knowledge to function effectively in administrative roles.

2. Multiple field experiences should be encouraged. This diversity permits interns to observe different leadership styles and gain clearer understandings of aspects of leadership that are unique to different school levels and those that are universally important. Cross-district internships can further broaden interns' perspectives.

3. Mentor and field supervisor roles should be made clear. Mentor relationships, as noted, involve an activity that goes beyond normal site supervision. It is an important role and should be clarified. Similarly, the field supervisor's role must be understood and agreed on by all parties. Beyond role definition, to make this role function as effectively as possible, sufficient site visits must be made to provide guidance for the formation of goals and plans, activities must be conducted in pursuit of these plans, and results must be meaningfully evaluated. Adequate training must be provided for mentors and field supervisors if these roles are to be conducted effectively.

4. Opportunities for reflection time are vital for interns to learn from their experiences in the field. Personal reflection must be cultivated. In addition, the more students can explore meaning through reflection with peers and others, the more that they can make sense of their experiences. Experiences are accumulated with great rapidity at the field-based sites, so opportunities to share reflections should be provided with regularity. Weekly or at least biweekly reflection sessions are required for this to happen.

Cohorts

Traditional programs admit students several times a year and offer courses in a cafeteria-style fashion, which makes it almost impossible to promote and maintain cohorts. Even when such programs are presented in some sort of sequence, there is no way to ensure that cohorts will develop, given differences in pacing with which students move through them.

All Danforth-related programs admit students to their experimental programs at established times, typically for summer or fall matriculation. The deliberate attempt to create cohorts has turned out to be one of the more important elements of the preparation process.

Each of the five universities goes about promoting cohorts in its own way. Alabama presents all academic work exclusively for program members, in an intensive 10-week session during the first summer of the program. Plans to establish a bridging class will bring the cohort onto campus for a full week during both the fall and spring semesters. At Central Florida, one or two courses per semester are reserved exclusively for program members, to promote group development. Extracurricular Renaissance activities bring members together to share a variety of unique experiences. Connecticut limits most of its courses to cohort members and also brings the group together once a month for a reflective seminar. Fresno's courses are limited to program members who also participate in frequent daylong workshops on current topics in administration. Washington has an intensive residential session aimed at group and team development during the first summer of the program, courses limited to program members, weekly reflection seminars, and an intensive week of synthesizing activities during the culminating summer.

COHORTS: CRITICAL ELEMENTS

Lessons for other institutions include the following:

1. At the program-management level, cohort development is important. It permits the coordinator to plan for student recruitment and selection, and later for placement as interns, in a cyclical and therefore more efficient manner. It also facilitates the purposeful sequencing of courses.

2. At the human learning and growth level, cohort development promotes support systems and networking among members of the student group. In fact, the cohort concept is becoming one of the mainstays of these programs, as the recognition grows that there is strength in numbers, particularly for participants in complex, innovative, and demanding programs.

3. Cohorts encourage long-term support systems, as graduates help each other to identify and seek administrative positions and provide a sympathetic ear and a source of suggestions for leadership behavior in difficult situations once positions are obtained. Many close lifetime friendships are also forged as a result of these intensive interactions.

4. The cohort approach provides a model of how schools can be transformed into adult learning communities. Cohort members who share in this powerful experience recognize how this unique learning approach can be transferred to the school site. They have experienced empowerment as adult learners and are more aware of the need to practice collaborative leadership as school administrators.

Program Management and Coordination

In the past few years, these five universities have focused on improving their preparation programs, particularly the field experience portions of those programs. Formerly, these preparation programs were organized in supermarket fashion. Like food shoppers, potential students, seeing little differences among preparation programs, chose one over another because of geographical convenience. Courses were developed and put on the shelf in hopes of attracting consumers who filtered through the program aisles at different rates of speed and with different degrees of enthusiasm about purchasing shelved items. Relatively speaking, only a few consumers bothered to engage in hands-on field experiences.

The new programs include such complex oversight activities as (a) active recruitment, (b) admission of students in cohorts, (c) development of academic experiences that are grounded in reality and presented in an interactive style that is coherent and sequential, and (d) promotion of enriched internship experiences for students. These activities require much more management and coordination. Where part-time attention to these responsibilities sufficed in the past, the expansion of activities has required significant program supervision and coordination.

All five of the universities have struggled with this issue as they deal with rapid rates of program growth and with the increasing complexity of program designs. Each, in its own way, has had to cope with issues such as the following:

- What kind of leadership is needed to ensure effective coordination?

- How can program continuity be established when there is leadership turnover?
- How can a meaningful reward system be created for those who take on this role?
- How can adequate clerical support be provided at a time when there are few, if any, new resources?

The University of Alabama has had four program coordinators. The first two served for 2 and 3 years, respectively. Both were senior faculty members with extensive prior experience as school administrators and had extensive networks with educational leaders in the field. The current co-coordinators, who are overseeing programs at different sites, are experienced school administrators, but they are also junior faculty members who have to cope with achieving tenure. As newcomers to the state, they also have to scramble to establish networks with field leaders. Some course-load reduction is built in for coordination responsibilities, but no new clerical staff has been provided.

At Central Florida, the initial coordinator left the university 3 months after the program began. His faculty replacement, a principal from the area, became co-coordinator for the rest of the year with the senior faculty member who proposed the program. She is coordinator of the current group, but next year, another newly appointed faculty member will be the coordinator. Neither of these faculty members is tenured, and no clerical support staff has been secured.

Originally, a senior faculty member with many field contacts was asked to serve as coordinator at Connecticut. Within a few months of the program's initiation, he was joined by a newly appointed faculty member, a former site-based administrator, who has since taken over this activity. She gets load credit for the task but has also been assigned other additional responsibilities, despite the fact that she still must achieve tenure. Recently, she was given 10 hours per week of graduate assistant time to support the coordination needs.

At Fresno, coordination is the responsibility of the senior faculty member who created the program. Although tenured, he is new to the area and has had to create a network of partner school superintendents to get the program started. In addition, he is the unit head for educational administration, so much of his program-coordination efforts are done as overload activity.

The first year of the program at the University of Washington was rather chaotic, as no one individual was responsible for coordination of the program. Since that time, a doctoral student with extensive experience as a school administrator has filled this role. When she completes her dissertation, a decision will have to be made concerning the employment of a new coordinator.

PROGRAM MANAGEMENT AND COORDINATION:
CRITICAL ELEMENTS

Four lessons for other institutions are worth noting:

1. Practitioner-scholars are needed to fill program-coordinating roles. These individuals must have legitimacy with field leaders and must understand the learning needs of interns at school sites. They must also be sensitive to academic program needs and be able to make contributions to that program. These distinctive attributes are not widely available. They are most likely to be found among successful educational administrators who also have shown an interest in continuing professional development, conducting research, and writing for publication. These rare individuals are most likely to be able to bridge the large gaps that frequently exist between universities and school districts.

2. Tenure criteria do not usually give serious consideration to service activities such as coordination of field-based programs. These criteria must be reviewed and modified appropriately to reward rather than punish those who take on this role. The activity is of value to the university, and those who manage it should be given appropriate credit for their efforts. This is not a recommendation to excuse coordinators who are on tenure tracks from doing research and publishing. However, the balance of research and publishing with service must be reconsidered for these role players. It may be more appropriate to define the coordinator's role as a clinical professorship, which

could be either a tenure-track line, if coordination activities leave time for research and publication, or a nontenure-track line if coordination is intended to be a full-time activity.

3. Adequate load reduction must be provided for this complex and demanding coordinating activity. Working with the many partners involved, guiding students through the many challenges they confront, and overseeing the processing of paperwork that goes with the effort, are major time-consuming responsibilities. They are responsibilities that require appropriate load reduction if they are going to be accomplished effectively.

4. Sufficient support personnel must be secured to process clerical activities (e.g., recruitment literature, admissions procedures and student files, internship placement information, communications, and evaluations) that keep the program afloat. In cases where no new resources are accessible, there must at least be reasonable efforts to redistribute existing support personnel time and availability. Field-based programs require constant attention and sufficient support personnel who process tasks and report to the coordinator.

Resources

Field-based preparation programs in educational administration require substantially more resources than do traditional preparation programs. Field-based programs demand richer funding for the following reasons:

1. Extensive coordination is necessary for the various phases of the program—recruitment, selection, admissions, program management, internship placement, supervision, evaluation, and assistance in obtaining initial placement. Depending on the size and complexity of the program, these activities require the full- or part-time attention of one or more faculty members.

2. Support personnel and space must be provided to enable coordinators to function effectively.

3. Release time must be made available so that students can be excused from their regular duties to have concentrated periods of time for hands-on experiences working with site-based mentors.

4. Support must be made available to engage leading educational administrators as instructors to improve the academic curriculum and its delivery because effective academic programs require a balance between theory and practice.

5. Enrichment activities such as guest speakers, retreats, and attendance at professional conferences are costly but important learning elements, especially during the formative stages of leadership preparation.

Administrators of traditional programs rely on the generation of student tuitions to obtain necessary resources. Their goal is to show a bottom line of sufficient student credit hours to justify continued university support for the program and its faculty. Administrators of field-based programs must be much more aggressive about securing additional university funding, as well as resources from other key partners, such as students and school districts.

All five of the universities have taken full advantage of Danforth Foundation support to help initiate their programs. These funds have been useful in many ways, including bringing people together to plan programs and enabling faculty members from different Danforth-supported programs to get together to share concerns and ideas. This relatively small resource base has the distinct advantage of being free of institutional constraints that typically accompany university funding. For example, many universities place severe restrictions on the use of institutional funds for meetings that involve food or entertainment.

Each of the universities has attempted to expand its resource base beyond this common funding source to meet the needs of its field-based program. The University of Alabama provides load recognition for the coordinator, as well as institutional support in the form of student tuition payments that flow back to the unit to pay both faculty members from other parts of the university and practicing school administrators who teach in the program. In addition, students pay a materials-and-supplies fee to defray duplication and dissemination expenses. However, largely due to shrinking state budgets, there has been little success in securing school-district sponsorship of release time for internship activities.

School districts cooperating with the University of Central Florida also ran into recessionary budget cutting at the state level, causing them to back away from their original commitment to sponsor release time and summer pay for interns. Support for the innovative Renaissance strand is also in jeopardy, now that Danforth funding is coming to an end. The university has given some load reduction for the coordinator and permits program participants to use vouchers for tuition payments earned by supervising student teachers.

The faculty at the University of Connecticut also anticipated district support for release time, but like faculty at Alabama and Florida, they were disappointed as the state reduced its support of school-district budgets. However, school districts do pay half of their staff members' tuitions. The coordinator gets some load recognition for her efforts and has half of a graduate assistant's time to help conduct her activities.

At Fresno, participating school districts provided $2,000,000 for release time during the first 2 years of the program. However, as in the other states, with shrinking budgets, this support is no longer available. As a result, release time, which was originally full- or half-time, depending on the district, is now only for the 8 to 12 days of workshops that are part of the academic program. Finally, the coordinator gets no load reduction for his efforts.

The University of Washington has been an exception to this generally negative resource picture. School districts have maintained their commitment to provide sufficient release time for at least half-time internship experiences. Students pay for several weeks of residential experiences on campus during the initial summer of the program. The university provides 25% of the coordinator's salary and is extending its commitment to 100%. Other resources have also been made available, including college overhead funds and, until recently, return of tuition monies to the unit.

Each of the five universities is attempting to institutionalize its experimental program, but this requires an adequate and secure resource base. Without this base, the programs are in jeopardy of termination or, just as bad, continuing, but only in form, not in substance. It is unrealistic to believe that field-based preparation programs can be created, established, and institutionalized without an adequate resource base. The movement from a self-contained, campus-based program for leadership preparation, to one that is field-based and involves extensive coordination, can only come about if adequate resources are committed to the effort.

RESOURCES: CRITICAL ELEMENTS

Three implications for other preparation programs stand out:

1. Risk capital must be obtained, particularly at the initial stages of program planning and design. This is when partnerships must be developed and dialogues must be established and maintained. This early and tenuous period of time requires a small but important resource base to bring people together to create program purposes and designs. A variety of sources have to be tapped for funds, including grants by foundations, business partnerships, and university-generated funds.

2. Long-term university support must be committed. Program changes of this magnitude require institutional allocation of resources for purposes such as release time, coordination, support staff for the coordinator, space to house staff and records, and pay for adjunct instructors.

3. All partners who benefit should be expected to share the resource burden. These programs, if well executed, benefit all role players, who should therefore be expected to provide necessary resources. They benefit students because they obtain the insights, skills, and exposure needed to become educational leaders. They benefit school districts that can identify potential leaders and then observe program participants in action before deciding whether to hire them. They also get opportunities to participate in the shaping of the leadership behaviors and styles of the coming generation of administrators. They benefit state-level policy-making centers because they are demanding more appropriate and effective preparation of educational leaders. They benefit universities and colleges of education because they establish more positive institutional images in the educational community, promote

opportunities for additional partnerships, and increase opportunities for faculty members to conduct research. As beneficiaries of these programs, it is reasonable to argue that each of these role players should contribute resources to support the programs.

Institutionalization

At some point, field-based programs must be institutionalized. Otherwise, they will quickly become history and will not continue into the future. Too often, we develop interesting and important programmatic innovations, only to find that they do not persist because of

- Lack of resources
- Frustration or exhaustion on the part of program champions
- Program personnel moving on to other projects or other places
- Turnover among the key actors who provided initial protection and support
- Intense rear-guard actions initiated by those opposed to the new approach

INSTITUTIONALIZATION: CRITICAL ELEMENTS

Several factors are associated with successful efforts to move from identification of a set of needs and beliefs, to alternative ideas, pilot testing, implementation and program modifications, and, finally, to institutionalization. These factors include the following:

1. A genuine and publicly agreed-on concern about the efficacy of the existing preparation program on the part of the faculty, and a willingness to examine alternative approaches
2. A clear vision, meaningful purposes, and a basic agreement about the program design
3. Highly committed program coordinators who are capable, and who have positive reputations in school districts

4. Understanding and support from key players, such as college deans, school superintendents, and principals

5. Risk capital for such needs as the development of networks, recruitment of excellent candidates, support for planning and program change as needed, and implementation of alternative instructional delivery systems

6. Perhaps the most important—the courage to stay the course through the inevitable difficult times that will occur and the insight to make changes that improve the program and its impact on leadership preparation

In the process of institutionalizing an innovative program, caution must be raised about not compromising key program elements. For example, complying with university expectations for packaging academic experiences as specific and long-established student-credit-hour formulations can decrease the ability of the program to be responsive to students' learning needs. Similarly, responding to budgetary constraints by reducing requirements for the amount of time that interns are expected to be in the field can negatively affect students' growth and development as educational leaders.

Further, if institutionalization means eliminating the status-quo program, which it did in the present cases, other issues may arise:

1. The sponsorship and candidate selection system may be compromised as all individuals seeking preparation are processed through what were initially experimental program structures.

2. It may be difficult to promote and maintain cohorts if admission is permitted at multiple points in the year and/or students can self-select into courses at their own pace.

3. Field-based programs attract candidates who typically are more highly motivated than the other preparation program candidates. Admitting all candidates into the same program may lead to friction between these groups and pressures to reduce the intensity of the program.

4. Many students enter traditional preparation programs out of curiosity. Some drop by the wayside, while others continue on to become administrators. Requiring candidates to have the

commitment at the outset that is expected of field-based co-horts may, unfortunately, eliminate some shoppers who could become excellent candidates for leadership positions in education.

5. Today's new thinking may become tomorrow's conservative and rigid status quo. Given the rapidly changing environment in which educational leaders function, care must be taken to build an ongoing interest and capacity for change. Improvement of leadership preparation programs is becoming an on-going task.

Such problems can be handled, but only if careful consideration is given to the costs and benefits of making an innovative program design the only choice for preparation candidates. Institutionalization is, in short, a double-edged sword. It is critically important to ensure the continuation of important and proven innovations, but if the process is not closely monitored and guided, it can also compromise the intent, structure, and content of the program.

Each of the five universities has given consideration to the question of institutionalization. In fact, at four of them—Central Florida is not yet at this stage—the decision has been made to eliminate the prior program and move to a field-based program as the only preparation option. These important decisions were made at Connecticut after only 2 years, at Fresno after 3 years, at Washington after 4 years, and at Alabama after 5 years. Each became effective as of the summer or fall of 1992. This seems to point to an important reality: Before consideration of institutionalization can be taken seriously, at least several years of experimentation and modification with the program are necessary.

A Comparison of Traditional and Danforth-Related Field-Based Programs

More than 5 years have passed since the Danforth Foundation initiated its efforts to have a positive impact on the preparation of educational administrators. This is a relatively short period of time, particularly when measured against the time that the behavioral-science-based programs that currently dominate preparation have had to evolve since the 1950s. Even at this early point in the development of Danforth-type field-based programs, sufficient experience and knowledge exist to identify trends and to make relevant comparisons between the two types of programs.

These comparisons, as identified in Table 8.3, leave the unmistakable conclusion that there are distinct and important differences between the two types of programs. In most instances, field-based programs are more likely to strive to be as follows:

1. Selective concerning who is permitted to participate in them—Efforts are made to carefully choose students on the basis of leadership potential, and the process involves field leaders as well as university faculty members.

2. Designed to emphasize leadership development—Hands-on, proactive learning is more likely to dominate in the classroom and at internship sites; students are challenged to test their capacity as leaders and take risks to grow as necessary before taking on administrative roles.

3. Based on adult learning principles—Programs are being reshaped and sequenced in ways that promote adult learning and development; instruction is delivered in interactive and highly participative ways.

4. Experiential—Courses tend to emphasize case studies, role playing, simulations, and analyses of field experiences; internships, which are goal driven, often include the development of contracts between interns and their supervisors, and they emphasize direct administrative responsibility more than shadowing and observing.

5. Complex—Field-based programs are typically more complicated at all stages, from recruitment and selection to assistance with placement; as such, they require more planning and coordination.

6. Supported in many ways by a wide network of role players as partners in the effort—Field-based programs, by their very nature, require the participation and involvement of school-district leaders, site-based administrators, program alumni,

(Text continued on p. 214)

TABLE 8.3 Traditional and Danforth Field-Based Programs

Categories	Traditional	Field Based
Participant sponsorship	None, other than recommendation forms	Usually by district committee, superintendent and/or principal
Recruitment	None usually	By districts and university
Admissions	Review of file, which emphasizes academic potential and is typically limited to transcripts, recommendations, standard exams	File with academic potential evidence is supplemented by evidence of leadership potential (educational platform, essay on leadership, interviews, assessment centers)
Advisement	Relatively little at M.A. or Ed.S. level, and limited to university faculty members	Extensive by coordinator as well as by field and site supervisors
Coordination	Minimal—usually limited to course scheduling by chairperson	Extensive—includes all stages of the effort, recruitment to placement
Student progression through program	At individual pace and typically over 3 or 4 years	At a predetermined pace and typically over 15 months to 2 years
Student grouping	None except by chance	In cohorts and usually extends beyond classes to include reflective seminars and other settings
Student evaluation	Course grades and sometimes an oral or written exam at end of the program	Course grades, but also regular feedback by coordinator as well as field and site supervisors, student reflection, and end-of-program exams
Program evaluation	Usually when an external review occurs, to comply with requests for information, and done by faculty members	Regularly and involves students, alumni, field administrators, as well as faculty members
Placement	Minimal involvement by faculty, beyond maintaining job-related information	Active advisement and networking by coordinator with program graduates and hiring school districts

Resources	Provided by students (tuition) and university (salaries and overhead support)	Provided by students (tuition, materials, and supplies), university (salaries, overhead support, space, coordinator load reduction), school districts (release time funds)
Partnerships	University dominated if done at all, infrequent meetings	Broad based, toward equal roles in decision making, frequent meetings
Program design and development	By faculty and not typically reviewed often	Done collaboratively and modified on basis of feedback
Academic program	Emphasis on theory and content, deductive approach	Balance between theory and practice, inductive approach
Instruction	Didactic, with professor as knowledge giver and student playing a passive role; professors do most of instructing, usually as individuals	Adult learning oriented with student playing a proactive role; practitioners as well as professors as instructors, often in teams
Field experiences/internships	Not usually required; vary widely in quality and time on task	Integral part of program, effort to ensure high quality and sufficient time-on-task
Field supervision	Often haphazard and infrequent, responsibility without load reduction and done by junior or adjunct faculty	Planned visits done frequently, usually with load reduction and involving senior faculty members
Site supervision	Usually by chance or circumstances, with little or no preparation for the role	Carefully selected supervisors who are given training and encouraged to act as mentors

as well as faculty members, adjunct instructors, and current students; all of these partners can be called on to provide assistance and support for activities such as recruitment and selection, program design and delivery, and placement of graduates; if the program is to succeed, partnerships that emphasize advocacy and support are required.

Implications for the Future of Administrator Preparation

We are in a time of major ferment. The field-based preparation programs discussed in this book may presage the way educational leadership preparation will be conducted in the future. The 1990s will probably be remembered as the time when a major break was made with the preparation programs of the past, just as the behavioral science/theory movement radically altered educational administration preparation since the 1960s.

ENTHUSIASM PREVAILS

There is great excitement brewing at the universities included in the study. Site visits were not purposefully planned around specific program events, yet regardless of when the visits were made, there was a positive energy permeating the setting. Faculty members and field leaders were engaged in planning, sharing instructional ideas, and making changes to improve programs. This was the situation whether the program was in its second year or its fifth year.

Students were deeply engrossed in and energized with academic and field projects. They were involved with their peers, sharing with each other their enthusiasm, perplexities, anxieties, and frustrations. When asked to describe their programs metaphorically, with little prodding, students were able to capture the essence of their experience, such as, "It's transformational, like a metamorphosis, opening doors on perspectives and possibilities." Each of the following examples begins, "It's like":

- A jazz piece. It has central themes with room for improvisation and it writes itself as it is being played.

- Vitamins. It enriches your life!
- Being buried in the *Encyclopedia Britannica*.
- A wide-angle lens with a growing aperture.
- Being a spider building a web. The supports are the university, my colleagues, my mentor, and my principal.
- Being a flower waiting to bloom.
- Being a kindergarten student on her first field trip (without mom!).
- Being on a roller coaster ride.

These positive metaphors reflect a sense of enthusiasm, challenge, growth, and opportunity, responses not typically heard from students in more traditional preparation programs. They are the remarks of students who see value in what they are experiencing and the solid foundation it is giving them as they prepare to take on educational leadership roles.

Their sense of self and their belief in their ability to meet the challenges ahead of them as educational leaders is extremely positive. They see themselves as special. After all, they have sponsorship, and they have been selected for highly competitive programs that are challenging.

Evidence has not been collected that can prove whether these students are actually better than others. In fact, it may just be the Pygmalion effect; that is, they believe in their worth because of the different way they are treated, from initial selection through placement. The important thing is that they do, indeed, feel special and capable, qualities that are critically important as a foundation for the development of effective leadership.

INDEPENDENT INVENTIONS OF
UNIVERSAL TRUTHS

Each of the five field-based programs is unique, being created, designed, modified, and maintained to meet the specific contingencies that exist in its particular environment. Yet, although differences may appear large when viewed from afar, they are really variations on a common theme when viewed up close. In fact, concerns and modification efforts at each site are clearly aimed at establishing the same kinds of improvements. In short, similarities are more pervasive than differences. Briefly stated, across sites:

1. The mission is to identify individuals with potential as educational leaders and to provide them with preparation experiences that enhance this potential.
2. There is recognition that current preparation programs must be changed significantly for this to happen.
3. This requires breaking free of the constraining mind set that curriculum should be exclusively determined by university faculty members, and instruction should be delivered in narrowly defined time periods at university centers and mainly by faculty members.
4. The field component of the program is critically important to the learning process. As such, it should be structured in ways that ensure high-quality experiences and sufficient time-on-task.

PROFESSIONALIZATION OF EDUCATIONAL ADMINISTRATION

Medicine and law recognize the need to guide novices who aspire to become doctors and lawyers, through a series of increasingly complex and meaningful experiences that prepare them to join the ranks of professionals in their field. They also recognize that this process is intensive and lengthy, and requires substantial investment of resources on the part of all partners, and that many aspirants are not likely to make it through the process.

Efforts being made by faculty members, students, and educational leaders to develop field-based programs are shifting preparation toward the doctor/lawyer model. Inevitably, this will lead to increased professionalization of educational administration.

The educational leadership community is joining together to identify promising leaders for the future, to provide meaningful preparation programs that emphasize learning by doing, and to discriminate among candidates in the identification of who will move into leadership roles.

LIFELONG LEARNING

These field-based programs are as much about serving adult learners who recognize the need to pursue lifelong learning as they are about certification or licensure for educational administrators. Alumni are pressing coordinators to consider their need for continuing involvement in the learning process. They are asking to be considered as site supervisors and to be allowed to attend various program-sponsored events. They are also reporting a need for continuing learning opportunities as they make the transition into leadership positions. Some universities are responding by cooperating with school districts to develop a variety of induction experiences for program graduates. Finally, as another indicator of their interest in lifelong learning, many graduates are making application for advanced study at the doctoral level.

The same enthusiasm for lifelong learning is being reported by mentors. They recognize the wonderful opportunities for professional development: the chance to reflect on their leadership behavior patterns, to share the learning that their interns are experiencing, and to meet and converse with colleagues and university faculty members. The lifelong learning needs of these senior administrators are being well served by the process.

The point is that preparation can no longer be viewed as something that is engaged in exclusively before obtaining a leadership position. The human drive to grow and learn and the rapidly changing environment in which leaders perform their roles require a long-term perspective on preparation. This reality will challenge current approaches of universities that engage in educational leadership preparation.

In Conclusion

There is no way of ensuring that fledgling programs will survive to move from ideas to innovations and on to institutionalization. In fact, it is just as likely that they will not, given problems such as inadequate resources for release time, coordination, and support needs; faculty disinterest in changing programs; and little history of meaningful partnerships between field leaders and university personnel. Even with the added status and extra funding they received, some of the universities that joined the Danforth Foundation program have seen their experimental programs fall by the wayside.

To make the process work, all interested parties must be convinced that the program will lead to a win-win situation:

1. Students need to see their preparation programs as meaningful and relevant.
2. Faculty need to recognize that they can do a better job of preparing students and that they will have greater access to field sites, which will increase their knowledge base for teaching, research, and writing.
3. School districts need to understand that they will have a larger and more direct role in identifying and sharing in the preparation of the next generation of leaders.

With this combination of potential payoffs, and a willingness to stay the course for perhaps 5 years or more, the potential for creating and maintaining meaningful field-based programs is greatly increased.

Pushing the Edge

Peter T. Wilson

The role of this final chapter is to push the edge. In the preceding case studies, Milstein has done a superb job of capturing the context, achievements, and struggles of 5 of the 22 diverse principal preparation programs that constitute the Danforth Program for the Preparation of School Principals (DPPSP). His description, summary, and analysis of those programs, cast against the broader experience with all 22 sites over 6 years, provide a starting point to raise specific points about program weaknesses and to identify major challenges that lie ahead for all those working to improve leadership for our nation's schools.

The following issues are addressed in this chapter:

1. The need for an educational platform—an articulated set of purposes and values in principal preparation
2. The necessary knowledge base for our nation's school leaders: rationale for a constructionist and intervention-oriented knowledge base
3. The need for systemic change—mutual reform—of schools and university schools of education; the isolation of educational administration from the larger educational reform movement; the potential for collaborative school-based research; a broader view of professional development

4. Technology as it relates to curriculum and pedagogy
5. The need for integrated community services for children and families at risk; designing preparation programs to meet this need
6. One foundation's response to these issues: the Principals Preparation Network; the School Leaders Program for linking schools, universities, and community agencies to develop leaders that serve children and their families

Educational Platforms

In the preface, Milstein cites six of the changes called for in the 1987 University Council for Educational Administration (UCEA) report *Leaders for America's Schools*. The first one is, "Define effective educational leadership." Although virtually all DPPSP sites have attempted to define effective educational leadership, the definitions, by and large, do not go beyond the minimum of contrasting educational leadership with administrative management. (The University of Washington and California State University, Fresno, are exceptions.) There are two dimensions to this shortcoming: First, many programs have not addressed the issue systematically. They have not entered a meaningful and sustained dialogue with their school partners on the subject. Second, there is a failure to address fundamental questions of value and purpose.

If there is a critical flaw in the DPPSP, it is that too little attention has been given to the most basic issue—core values. Principal preparation must address the fundamental questions: "Leadership to what end?" "Schools for what?" and "For whom?"

Educational platforms articulate basic purposes and core values. They provide a basis for dialogue and a guide for action. Only moral leadership with explicit purpose and values provides the possibility for the kind of community dialogue requisite to improve our schools radically.

The preparation of school leaders for the 1990s and beyond must deal with the changing demographic and economic context of schooling, as well as the enduring problems of education for a democratic society. To move forward in the face of these profound changes and to be truly democratic in nature, educators will need moral leadership grounded in values congruent with this purpose.

For example, an area such as Fresno, California, cannot survive with a business-as-usual approach to education. Fresno is one of the fastest-growing areas in the country; a vast majority of the newcomers are migrant families. More than 80 languages are spoken in the metropolitan area. What does it mean to educate the children of the Fresno area, both newcomers and descendants of longtime residents, to be citizens for American democracy in the 21st century? Although Fresno is a stark case, the issues raised are relevant nationally, from the cities of the Northwest to the rural hollows of the Appalachians.

Many of our children bring to school complex problems that are not essentially educational but that directly affect their ability to find success in school. Language, culture, health, poverty, and abuse are issues that must be addressed. What are the implications for the preparation of school leaders? Each preparation program must rethink philosophy, goals, content, and delivery in light of these issues. These programs must produce leaders who can make a difference—who can help build schools that are effective for all children. Otherwise, university-preparation programs will not be able to justify continued existence, and other institutions will step in to do the job.

Value-driven program development is a far cry from the positivistic, management-driven paradigm that has dominated the profession for the past 40 years. A view of school leadership as a moral activity requires each preparation program to identify nonnegotiable core values as the basis for program development—in other words, to create an educational platform. All activities must be constantly assessed against this platform. Candidates must be involved in a similar process. Over time, we should be able to see these values manifested in the schools led by the programs' graduates.

What kind of core values should be involved? Perhaps the most essential is inclusion. *Inclusion* is a commitment to success for all children. Inclusion requires a new approach to cultural diversity. It means moving beyond the numerical approach of affirmative action. It means moving beyond valuing diversity to managing for diversity (Thomas, 1991). Inclusion demands that we build organizations in which people learn from difference and use difference to achieve individual and organizational goals.

Schools model another core value, *education for democracy*, by ensuring that all those with a stake in the child's education are active partners, including parents, teachers, school leaders, and community. The African proverb, "It takes a village to raise a child," must become a reality of schooling in America. Curriculum and instruction must stress active, critical citizenship, giving each child a sense of effectiveness, a confidence that she or he can act on the world, not just the other way around. Preparation programs must do the same for future school leaders. More than ever, democracy requires empowered citizens who are active, lifelong learners.

A third core value, *a constructionist view of knowledge*, defines our approach to learning and the relationship between teachers and students, both in our schools and in our universities. It is the foundation for creating a truly democratic citizenry.

Knowledge and the Knowledge Base

How we view the nature of knowledge informs most of what we do in education, whether consciously or unconsciously. Our approaches to teaching, learning, curriculum development, and organizational structure, and our view of the process of change for individuals and organizations are rooted in our knowledge paradigm. Therefore, we need to be aware of different views of knowledge and their implications, and we must consciously build curricula and human interactions with a view of knowledge that can support the core values of inclusion and democracy.

Disparate paradigms of knowledge inform the current work of preparing principals. In most cases, these differing views of knowledge affect preparation programs neither systematically nor intentionally. They become explicit only through the interest of an individual faculty member. Even then, epistemology is not consciously shaping more than an individual course.

For nearly half a century, the dominant paradigm (Murphy, 1992) guiding educational administration has been the behaviorist, positivistic paradigm. This paradigm drives and rationalizes organizations based on authority and control. It views decision making as an objective, value-free act, reinforces the status quo, and defines leadership as management. It legitimizes the dominant instructional practice of lecturing. When knowledge is viewed as inert, teaching is seen as handing something to the learner, as passing on an inert body of knowledge to passive learners. The teacher, as expert, is pouring knowledge into students.

Constructionism, in contrast, says that the learner must construct knowledge for him- or herself. The learner must make meaning or sense of the world. This view of knowledge is reflected in the Coalition of Essential School's motto, "Student as worker" (Sizer, 1992). It means that students must be at least as active as teachers. It requires an environment where risk taking is supported because constructing knowledge requires trial and error.

Constructionism changes the power relationship between teachers and learners—in fact, among everyone. The old view of knowledge equated teacher with expertise; expertise meant control. Constructionism empowers the learner, all learners. It sees the construction of knowledge as requiring not only individual reflection but also interaction with others. This view, that knowledge is constructed socially, has profound implications for classroom teaching and the organization of institutions, both schools and universities. Projected onto organizational theory, a constructionist view of knowledge requires a move from a hierarchical control structure to a flatter, more participatory structure.

For example, earlier, we discussed the need to restructure schools so that parents and community become active partners in the education of the child. This dramatic shift must take place at a time of insistent calls for increased professionalization of teachers and school leaders (Lieberman, 1988). When viewed from the perspective of top-down, expert-controlled, static knowledge, this need for a more inclusive educational partnership is incompatible with increased professionalization. By contrast, a constructionist view of knowledge values the richness of a broader partnership *and* recognizes the new skills and responsibilities required for its success.

Complementary Paradigms

The work of a number of educational theorists and practitioners relates to and complements the constructionist view of knowledge. This is not the place to examine these schools of thought. Rather, these brief sketches indicate the breadth and applications of work that together compose a radically different approach to thinking about teaching and learning, organizational and administrative leadership. Patrick Forsyth, executive director of the UCEA, addresses the nature of the knowledge base necessary for effective preparation of school leaders. He starts from the premise that this is preparation for a profession and that it therefore must be intervention oriented. It may well differ from the knowledge base required for a university researcher (Forsyth, 1992).

David Schon distinguishes technical rationality from reflection in action. Technical rationality is rooted in positivism and in the epistemology of academia. By contrast, reflection in action, like Forsyth's intervention orientation, is rooted in and about action. It is an epistemology of practice. Technical rationality, grounded in positivism, is reductionist and emphasizes convergent thinking. It assumes agreement about purpose, and so it applies technical means to solve clearly defined problems. Reflection in action sees the world of practice as messy, recognizing its complexity, instability, uniqueness, and value conflicts (Schon, 1983, p. 14). For Schon, problem setting must precede and inform problem solving. Problem setting requires the establishment of priorities based on values and experimentation.

The cognitive view, as described by Nona Prestine of the University of Illinois, recognizes context and complexity, the central role of people and their feelings, and an interactive relationship between thinking and action. This is in direct contrast to behaviorism and functionalism, which see the world as ordered and predictable, define problems abstractly, and view leadership narrowly and passively, as simply management (Prestine, 1991).

Ken Leithwood's work on expertise at the Ontario Institute for Studies in Education represents an important development of the cognitive view. Also of significance is the work of Ed Bridges of Stanford and Phil Hallinger of Vanderbilt on problem-based learning. They take problems from the complex lives of school leaders and engage learners in collaborative problem solving, using interactive simulations based on the effective-schools literature. These simulations make technology a tool for learning (Bridges [with Hallinger], 1992).

Poststructuralism, as defined by Louis Miron, rejects the depersonalized, objectified management approach of the previous era to assert the centrality of human agency. Poststructuralization is value driven, holds equity as the goal, and sees school leaders and the school community as the vehicle for achieving this goal. Leadership becomes a transformational, moral activity, which must overcome the bureaucratic demands that conserve the status quo (Miron, 1991).

The poststructuralist view is embodied in Henry Levin's Accelerated Schools model, now being implemented in over 200 schools around the country (Levin, 1990). The Accelerated Schools are grounded in locally created visions of education that empower the entire school community. They are driven by a collaborative inquiry process; the information generated by the school-based inquiry teams is primarily for the schools' own purposes, not merely for accountability to centralized bureaucracies.

Very close to the poststructuralists are the radical or critical educators such as Henry Giroux. They reject reductionism and discipline-based curriculum in favor of an interdisciplinary approach to creating a more democratic society. Highly political, they empower individuals and celebrate difference. Teachers engage in critical inquiry, which then informs curriculum development. The critical theorists' emphasis on context is consistent with the cognitive view. Giroux connects modernism, postmodernism, and feminism as postcolonial frameworks contributing to a movement to transform the legacies of the colonial world. This is a deliberately political approach to education (Giroux, 1992).

The Learning Organization conceptualized by Peter Senge explicitly builds on the constructionist view. It shares the poststructuralist view of knowledge and connects this specifically with Edward Demming's total quality management. Both Demming and Senge share the critical educators' view of collaboration and emphasize the role of dialogue in the construction of knowledge and meaning (Senge, 1990).

The readiness of the field to explore these activist, intervention-oriented approaches was encouragingly demonstrated at the April 1992 National Forum on Problem-based Learning for Educational Leadership Programs cosponsored by the Danforth Foundation and the National Policy Board for Educational Administration. The sizable turnout and the enthusiasm for a day and a half of hands-on workshops suggest that a significant cadre of educational-administration faculty see the need for change and are eager for help in working with new tools.

Systemic Change

An educational platform grounded in inclusion, democratic education, and a constructionist view of knowledge demands systemic change. As Peter Senge would say, it requires "systems thinking." The need for systemic change contrasts markedly with the isolation of educational administration from the broad arena of school reform and restructuring.

This lack of connection mirrors the anachronistic departmentalization within schools of education. It reflects the behavioral-science knowledge base that has dominated the profession for the past half century. By contrast, preparation programs grounded in an intervention-oriented knowledge base integrating work from the aforementioned several schools of thought could be a powerful force for transformation of our nations' schools and preparation programs. We must broaden the focus of reform efforts to encompass the simultaneous reform of schools, teacher education, educational administration and schools of education. A brief examination of the Professional Development School (PDS) phenomenon bridging teacher education and school restructuring underscores this point.

Since the mid-1980s, several major studies have proposed the creation of PDSs. These studies have spurred a reform movement in teacher education targeted at systemic change of both schools and university teacher education programs. The two largest efforts, in terms of funding base and numbers of active sites, are the Goodlad School Renewal Network and the Holmes Group. In addition, the

American Association of Colleges of Teacher Education (AACTE), the National Education Association (NEA), and the American Federation of Teachers (AFT) each support several PDS efforts.

In addition to the PDS partnerships, other overall school-district restructuring and site-based management efforts are being attempted throughout the country. These include Ted Sizer's Coalition of Essential Schools, the related statewide ReLearning projects, Henry Levin's Accelerated Schools Program, Mastery in Learning Consortium, Ed Ziegler's Schools of the 21st Century, and mandated reforms in Kentucky and Chicago. A number of DPPSP sites have tried to influence and/or be a part of such efforts (East Tennessee State University, Virginia Tech University, Brigham Young University, University of New Mexico, University of Washington, and University of Alabama).

Several dimensions of the PDS and related efforts bear watching by those involved in the preparation of school leaders: (a) partnerships committed to the mutual and concomitant reform of the university and the schools, (b) the central role of inquiry, and (c) a broader view of leadership.

Mutual Reform of
University Programs and Schools

PDS partnerships are committed to reforms that exceed those of most DPPSP programs, specifically, to mutual and concomitant reform of both schools and universities. In contrast, in most DPPSP partnerships, the reform focus has been primarily on the principal preparation program, without major emphasis on concomitant reform of the schools. (Exceptions are California State University, Fresno, and the University of Washington, which have tied mutual reform of area school districts to radical changes in the university preparation program.)

DPPSP also has been focused quite narrowly on principal preparation rather than on the broader field of administrator preparation. At a number of DPPSP sites, however, reform of the principals preparation program is leading to reform of other programs within educational administration (e.g., doctoral programs at University of Tennessee, East Tennessee State University, Virginia Tech University, University of New Mexico, and University of Washington).

Both the DPPSP and PDSs are calling for a reexamination of appropriate roles and activities for faculty in the universities and in the schools. In Chapter 8, Milstein raises the need to experiment with alternative roles. Miller and Walters document the blurring of roles in PDSs in the Southern Maine Partnership (National Center for Restructuring Education, Schools and Teaching [NCREST] case study, in press). A number of PDSs are experimenting with clinical faculty and/or university and school-based teacher educators. Other alternative roles include mentors, coaches, team teachers, and collaborators in school-based research.

The semantic innovation of referring to both university and school staff as faculty rather than school "teachers" and university "faculty" implies larger issues. These include empowerment and the flattening of hierarchical organization. PDSs aim to reframe the school/university relationship from the traditional one of university as source of expertise and controller of teacher education to a partnership of equals.

The Central Role of Inquiry

Experimentation with new roles also reflects a commitment to inquiry as central to mutual reform. Ann Lieberman, in her American Educational Research Association Presidential Address (1992), advocated an alternative research paradigm built on a constructionist view of knowledge and collaborative inquiry. One of the major outcomes of collaborative school-based research is a marriage of research and practice. Research informs practice, and practice informs research.

Collaborative research between school and university teachers challenges the view of research as the exclusive domain of the individual professor. So does another aspect of the new research paradigm: the possibility of departmental research agendas to support a programmatic commitment (e.g., a professional development school). This would require some compromise of the traditional faculty prerogative of academic freedom (e.g., it could require each faculty member to commit some portion of her or his time to a common research project).

Clinical faculty and school-based collaborative research programs run counter to the current culture of both schools and universities. Real work in schools is messy. Research is hard to control and invariably time consuming. Milstein raises related concerns about the time commitment required for team teaching and for managing the complexity of collaborative school-based university programs.

New roles incorporating collaborative activity will require major revisions in the reward and promotion structures of both universities and schools. These structures currently reward publication, particularly of single-authored research, with only secondary value assigned to teaching and service. Increased value must be placed on collaborative work, both as team teaching and joint research. The time-consuming and complex nature of developing and managing field-based programs must be recognized, allotted adequate time and resources, and rewarded.

If inquiry becomes central to the collaborative work of the school and the university, what are the implications for school leadership? What does it mean for school organization, management style, professional development, instructional leadership? If inquiry is central to the work of the school and teachers are involved in action research, how will this affect the relationship between teachers and university faculty, and between faculty and students?

If the line between teachers and university faculty is blurred, how does this affect the role of the principal? Traditionally, principals have exercised control by limiting access to information in a hierarchical organization. Teachers engaged in action research, creating knowledge, and collaborating directly with university faculty will be empowered. They will require a new kind of leader, one who is empowering and enabling.

How will the participation in action research by candidates in principal preparation programs affect the process and content of those programs?

A Broader View of Leadership and
the Professional Development Continuum

School/university partnerships must reconceptualize leadership and professional development. Professional development has been too narrowly defined. Preservice preparation of teachers and pre-service preparation of principals are unrelated, both conceptually and programmatically; preservice and in-service education are similarly compartmentalized. We need to see all four as components of a continuum of professional development. Leadership development must be integrated at all levels if we are to develop effective site-based school management with empowered, professional staff.

INDUCTION

The reform reports of the mid-1980s focused attention on the period of professional induction for both teachers and principals (see for example, Carnegie Forum on Education and the Economy, 1986). This issue has now been taken up by state policy makers and professional organizations. There is increasing evidence that effective preparation programs are not enough. A good beginning, encompassing the first year or two of work, is also essential. A trained mentor who is readily accessible for on-site support and observation is critical. If schools and universities form partnerships based on mutual ownership of professional development, a continuum of professional preparation induction and development is more likely to be realized.

MENTOR TRAINING AND MENTORS

Mentors say that mentor training and, particularly, serving as a mentor are powerful professional-development activities. However, DPPSP preparation programs have generally viewed mentoring as only the means to an end: enriching internships for preparation candidates. Mentor training and mentor experiences and relationships have been neglected as opportunities for the professional development of experienced practitioners.

COHORT GROUPS AND NETWORKS

One final aspect of professional development should be mentioned. Danforth preparation programs admit students in cohorts because of the impact that the cohort grouping has on student learning and student/faculty relations. The cohort breaks down the isolation of students from each other. The cohort empowers students in the student/faculty relationship at the same time that it facilitates closer, more supportive student/faculty ties.

The power of the cohort need not be lost after students complete their program. The graduates, as a cohort, constitute a natural network. The power of professional networks has been well documented by Lieberman and McLaughlin (1992). Several sites in the Danforth program provide some vehicle for gathering graduates on an occasional basis. The response has been enthusiastic.

Networking is helpful to current students, also. The Danforth Principals Program Network, a network of the 20 active Danforth sites, included interns in a recent meeting of the eastern region universities. The interns were vocal about how positive they found this experience. They especially valued seeing their programs as part of a national movement.

Networks protect individuals from feeling isolated who are attempting change. Equally important, networks provide essential opportunities for professional dialogue. The common ground of shared values and goals provides the trust and psychological safety necessary for dialogue. Individual differences and contexts provide the basis for challenging one another. Challenge in a safe environment is critical for continued personal and organizational change.

TECHNOLOGY

Most preparation programs have taken little advantage of the extraordinary advances in available technology. A short list of the many easily accessible applications includes video for documentation in student portfolios; computers for word processing and budget simulations; modems for long-distance electronic networking (e.g., between candidates and/or mentors); and teleconferencing, particularly with geographically dispersed populations. (Iowa State, University of Wyoming, and Virginia Tech University are experimenting with electronic networks, and Virginia Tech makes regular use of teleconferencing.)

More sophisticated applications hold enormous potential. Interactive computer simulations, enhanced with Hypercard and CD-ROM (compact disk—read-only memory) technology, allow preparation programs to simulate complex experiences that cannot be planned for in on-site internships. Excellent examples of available software are the ITCOT simulation from Vanderbilt University and Instructional Leadership: Interactive Video Disk Instruction from Leadership Studies Inc., 1988, currently being used by East Tennessee State University.

Equally important is the incorporation of technological literacy into preparation program curricula. Computer competence in word processing, budgeting, and planning should be basic skills taught in each program. School leaders need to be literate in a wide range of educational technology applications, including curricular and instructional applications.

SERVING THE WHOLE CHILD

Educating all children requires that we serve the whole child, including the social, cultural, intellectual, emotional, and physical, because the conditions for learning are affected by all these factors. We could not separate out the intellectual and effectively educate even if a purely intellectual education was our goal. However, our goals, our core values, are far more expansive. For example, mental and physical health, a sense of well-being, must be addressed if we are to educate for empowerment. For the 25% of our nation's children who live in poverty, and for those who experience violence in their personal lives or for whom family nurturance is not a given, we must intervene in conjunction with educating to empower both children and families to become democratic citizens.

The recognition that we must provide support for the whole child if she or he is going to have a successful school experience leads directly to the need to provide integrated community services for children and their families. Reality-based problems of educating the whole child are inherently interdisciplinary. Many of the problems facing school leaders today require the knowledge and perspective of a cross-disciplinary, interprofessional team, broader than can be found within a school of education, public health, nursing, or social work. We need to radically reexamine professional education in the helping professions.

What are the implications for the preparation of teachers, principals, and central office personnel? What new skills, knowledge, and attitudes will each of these professionals require? Similarly, what are the implications for the other professionals—the social workers, physical, and mental health providers? What will linking their services to schools imply for their training?

In the Danforth Foundation's plans for the future, looking at the issues raised in this chapter and in Milstein's analysis of the five sites (Chapter 8), the Danforth Foundation decided in 1991 to change the emphasis of its work on preparation of school leaders. Two key decisions were made:

First, to redirect work in DPPSP from supporting the development of new sites to building a network of existing sites, the Principals Preparation Network. Foundation staff members recognized that the 20 active programs, while constituting only 5% of all programs nationally, and although in the early stages of development, were having a significant impact on the field. This was obvious in the literature, at conferences and national meetings, and in the many inquiries about the DPPSP. However, it was equally clear that this work had only begun to scratch the surface. Foundation resources were reorganized into the Principals Preparation Network to meet the following goals: (a) to provide continued support through the opportunity for program staffs to meet with others pursuing the same ends; (b) to deepen the understanding of what constitutes an effective principal preparation program and what strategies are most effective in implementation; (c) to explore ways to open the network to others involved in similar program development; and (d) to pursue other means of documenting and disseminating the work.

Second, the Danforth Foundation made a multiyear commitment to a new initiative, the School Leaders Program. The School Leaders Program is working with four university/school/community partnerships committed to creating school success for every child. The foundation sought partnerships to lead mutual reforms of teacher education, principal preparation and professional induction, and K-12 education. At the same time, the partnerships are launching innovative collaborations between schools and community agencies. It is expected that the partnerships will learn much from each other and will have much to share with the field as a whole. In a related development, the Stuart Foundations and the Casey Foundation are supporting an initiative on Interprofessional Training jointly housed at the University of Washington and California State University-Fullerton. The hoped-for outcome from all these efforts are better educated, healthier children and families, and a more truly democratic society.

In Closing

As the 20th century draws to a close, crisis looms. Our institutions are geared to the myths of the traditional family, a classless society and white male Western values. Yet, 25% of our nation's children under the age of 6 years live in poverty. Racial tensions grow. We have only begun to experience what will be drastic demographic changes toward a much larger percentage of older, predominantly European-American citizens, and a school- and working-age population that will approach 50% people of color. The so-called traditional family with two parents, working father, homemaker mother, and two children represents only 17% of today's American families.

In the face of these conditions, schools cannot cater only to "those who can," hanging on to the status quo. Schools must serve all children. Schools must not only transmit our tradition of democratic values but also empower individuals to be active democratic citizens. Programs to prepare leaders for our nation's schools, as Milstein's five cases illustrate, have begun to change rather dramatically how we prepare leaders for our schools. However, we must push for more radical change. We must change not only how we prepare leaders for our nation's schools, but also why.

References

Bridges, E. M. (1992). *Problem based learning for administrators*. Eugene, OR: ERIC Clearinghouse, Educational Management.

Carnegie Forum on Education and the Economy. (1986). *A nation prepared: Teachers for the 21st century—The report of the task force on teaching as a profession*. New York: Author.

Forsyth, P. (1992, February). *Knowledge in educational administration: Problems of practice defined*. Paper presented at the meeting of the Danforth Program for the Preparation of School Principals, Western Regional Meeting, San Diego, CA.

Giroux, H. (1992). *Border crossings: Cultural workers and the politics of education*. New York: Routledge, Chapman and Hall.

Levin, H. M. (1990). *Building school capacity for effective teacher empowerment: Application to elementary schools with at-risk students*. Stanford, CA: Stanford University Press.

Lieberman, A. (Ed.). (1988). *Building a professional culture in schools*. New York: Teachers College Press.

Lieberman, A. (1992, April 22). *The meaning of scholarly activity and the building of community*. Presidential speech delivered at the annual meeting of the American Educational Research Association.

Lieberman, A., & McLaughlin, M. W. (1992, May). Network for educational change: Powerful and problematic. *Phi Delta Kappan, 73*(9), 673-677.

Miller, L., & Walters, S. (in press). *Professional development schools: Schools for developing a profession*. New York: Teacher's College Press.

Miron, L. F. (1991, Fall). The dialectics of school leadership: Post-structural implications. In *Organizational theory dialogue*. Unpublished manuscript, University of San Diego.

Murphy, J. (1992). *The landscape of leadership preparation: Reframing the education of school administrators*. Newbury Park, CA: Corwin.

Prestine, N. A. (1991, Fall). Problem solving and expertise: A cognitive view of administrative leadership. In *Organizational theory dialogue*. Unpublished manuscript, University of San Diego.

Schon, D. A. (1983). *The reflection practitioner: How professionals think in action*. New York: Basic Books.

Senge, P. (1990). *The fifth discipline*. New York: Doubleday.

Sizer, T. (1992). *Horace's school: Redesigning the American high school*. New York: Houghton Mifflin.

Thomas, R. (1991). *Beyond race and gender*. New York: Amacom Press.

University Council for Educational Administration. (1987). *Leaders for America's schools*. College Station, PA: Author.

Index